I HAVE WHAT IT TAKES

STORIES AND PRINCIPLES THAT WILL IGNITE YOUR NATURAL LEADERSHIP

BY
MARTHA HERNÁNDEZ | ESTELA LOPEZ |
ANDREA GUENDELMAN | FLOR MELARA |
MARILU GONZALEZ | MIROSLABA VELO |
OVI VÁSQUEZ

Top Leadership Experts

I HAVE
WHAT
IT TAKES

INTRODUCTION

It makes me happy to know you are reading this book. I hope the following stories from people who have transformed their own lives will help you transform yours. If you are so busy that you don't have time to read the whole book, then read at least one story, and I promise you it will be worth it.

I handpicked each of the leaders who I invited to share their stories in this book. I selected them because I know their lives can impact you in a positive way. The entrepreneurs, leaders, business owners, and educators who are part of this book truly amaze me. In fact, after reading each of their chapters, I felt like I needed to get coached by each one of them for at least six months. It's truly remarkable what each of them has to offer, and I am really honored that they decided to do this book along with me.

I put this idea together because I know my people (*mi gente*), like you are seeking out one more piece of advice that might ignite the fire in you to take your leadership game to the next level so you can win. And you can win the game, not just for yourself but for all your team, which also means our whole community.

I hope you enjoy this book and connect with each one of us, or at least connect with one of us who you most identify with. We are all very happy to hear what it is you felt during the time you decided to invest in this book, because we truly believe we can be a great resource for someone like you to achieve a higher level of success. We shared our stories to show you where we came from, and we shared our principles to show you how we got to where we are now. The number of principles shared by each author varies because we all approach success from a different angle according to what is available to us at the moment of making a decision, using different resources and having a different level of awareness.

Strategy is everything, and the story means everything.

—Ovi Vásquez, StudentSuccessExpert.com
In February 2019, I got accepted to
Harvard Business School Online.

CONTENTS

Martha Hernández, Founder and CEO, madeBOS, Inc.

Martha Hernández, quit her executive career and founded madeBOS, an AI platform that helps employers untap overlooked employees and makes it possible to retain and empower them through a proprietary technology that focuses on a proven career pathing methodology that Martha developed. "The day I understood my power I committed myself to utilizing it to the empowerment of others. I understood that in order to achieve greatness, it didn't matter how far I had come but how hard I was willing to work to go the farthest I could."

Estela Lopez, Living Compass Community Wellness Advocate and Entrepreneur.

"Estela Lopez is passionate about helping people become the best version of themselves to live an abundant life through goal-setting, personal growth, and behavior modification. Estela is a leader, who believes in multiplying leaders and their skills."

Adrea Guendelman, Harvard Law School LL.M., Director of Inclusive Innovation at CU Boulder, Founder of BeVisible Latinx and most recently Wallbreakers

"Andrea left a successful career as a Harvard-trained corporate lawyer for the risky journey of an entrepreneur. Her latest startup, Wallbreakers, combines her passion for opening doors for women and young people from underrepresented communities with her mission to diversify elite and exclusive industries such as tech, finance, and media. Her quest to connect these communities draws inspiration from her immigrant grandfather's business, where he sold to communities the rest of his country ignored."

Flor Melara, M.S. in Communications, Executive Television Producer.

"Understanding the hardships of life and learning to turn those obstacles into testimonies that can impact and motivate someone to try again is what Flor Melara aims to achieve with her story of perseverance and determination. Learning to voice her opinion, she has become a young leader who became an executive producer in less than two years, working for one of the largest media companies in the United States."

Marilu Gonzalez, M.A. in Educational Leadership, Coach and Keynote Speaker

"Coach 'Marilu' Gonzalez has spent the last ten years building a competitive Women's Soccer Program. Coach Marilu has been part of the soccer community since 1994. Soccer is her passion, but coaching is her life. She is a graduate from Chicago State University and Concordia University, where she earned a B.S. in Physical Education and M.A. Educational Leadership respectively. Coach Marilu describes her philosophy as "applying all team skills to real-life situations and expecting excellence on and off the field."

Miroslaba "Lili" Velo-Egonmwan, M.A. in Educational Leadership, Author and Speaker

"Miroslaba Velo-Egonmwan has been an educator for over fifteen years and currently serves as assistant principal at an urban high school in northern California. She is passionate about creating opportunities for students to identify their purpose-driven life by sharing her personal journey."

Ovi Vásquez, National Keynote Speaker, Author & Founder of StudentSuccessExpert.com

"Ovi went from a farm boy, raised in a poor village in the sugarcane fields of Central America, to being accepted to Harvard Business School Online. He is the author of five books and a Univision On-air collaborator. Ovi has worked for global corporations like Apple, Tesla, Salesforce, and Uber.

Ovi is a role model for first-generation college students. He educates and connects with students by sharing his story and insights on how they can succeed in school. Through social media, Ovi has helped thousands of students nationwide. He has shared over $750,000 in scholarships for minority students. He emerges today as one of the most sought-after bilingual youth leadership speakers of our time."

Thank you! ....**Page 139**

CHAPTER 1

MARTHA HERNÁNDEZ

From Nopalera[1]* to CEO

*W*ould *you like to buy nopales*[2]±*?* That was my phrase when I was six years old. I was a businesswoman even then with my bucket of nopales in my hand, shouting outside my house. Three knocks, a shout, "Would you like to buy nopales?" and thousands of laughs that echoed in the corridor directly from the kitchen. My mother and my aunts, with tears in their eyes, almost dead with laughter, would open the door and we'd repeat

---

[1]* nopalera: a woman who sells Mexican cactus
[2]± a Mexican cactus

the sales delivery over and over and fine tune it until it was bullet proof, at least for a six year old. They innocently encouraged my entrepreneurial spirit.

After selling nopales, I leveled up to sell tangerines, then chickens, and I even had a stage where I tapped into my inner artist and made bows for girls' hair. I, without shame, sold them at family parties. It was my joy to help my mother, since my father, who worked in the fields of Salinas, California, and Yuma, Arizona, mysteriously disappeared one day and stopped sending us money.

My world changed when I heard my mom secretly tell a family member that I was born in the United States. I immediately asked questions, but the only thing I could get out of them was "Silly, don't tell anyone, because the Americans will take you." Confused, I remember that I didn't know whether to feel distressed or liberated. I loved my life in my little town, Chavinda, Michoacán, but I also wanted to go to "El Norte." In my town almost everyone I knew aspired to go to the United States.

When my mom finally decided to return to the United States, I was super excited and didn't understand why my aunts, who were left behind, cried so sadly watching the van in which we were going to disappear. The three-day trip quickly turned into more than a week. The van we were traveling in broke down halfway there, and we had to leave it behind. I remember we took out the few things we brought and finished the journey to the border by bus. I crossed the border with an uncle while my mom and my sisters risked their lives through the desert. The danger they faced never crossed my mind. My uncle, whom I knew very little about, and I, once in American soil, waited at a McDonalds for many hours until, finally, a relative I had never seen before came to pick us up. I was nine years old, and yet I didn't cry or ask questions; I just waited.

When we got in the car, the man told my uncle that my mom and my sisters had been caught by the *migra*, but they tried a second time and successfully crossed the border. What a relief! My uncle and I still had more than twelve hours to go, but that didn't matter to me because the four of us were in California already.

Although I didn't know how to navigate the educational system, much less speak English, I felt safe, as if I finally was on the land to which I belonged. That fantasy was short-lived. In just weeks, I remember cries of despair, begging my mom to return us to Mexico. It took months, but finally, my mom promised to return us to Chavinda, stating, "We're leaving — but not for five years."

Although it wasn't the expected answer, there was hope. I took courage and put all my effort into life in the United States. Unfortunately, in Oakland, California, in the 90s, even if I gave it my all, Latinos were very few, and we suffered a lot of marginalization. Girls of other races bullied me and even threatened to take away my belongings. Sadly, I stopped carrying pencils, notebooks, and anything of value. Can you believe that one day I even lost my shoes? I lost them while running from a group of boys who were angry for some reason and tried to beat us. I didn't know what was going on, but suddenly all the Latinos started running with the non-Latinos chasing after them. They beat up those who were left behind. I jumped over a metal wall and ended up beaten, without shoes, at a classmate's house who lived near school.

What very few know is that the hardest thing for me was not the assaults and racial discrimination at school but the mocking of my own family and friends when they found out that my dad collected aluminum cans to support us. That didn't embarrass us because we understood how hard it was for my dad to find a job. He didn't speak English, although he came to the United States when he was a teenager;

he never needed it working in the fields. He also didn't know how to drive because he spent most of his youth under the influence of alcohol. He didn't feel capable of learning something new because he was mentally recovering from more than five years of being homeless. He'd been a beggar, lost on the streets of Arizona, who didn't even know his own name.

Surprisingly, I never held a grudge against anyone since I recognized that they acted like that due to the lack of resources and opportunities. I remember very well that at my Quinceañera mass, in front of a crucifix, I fully committed to God and asked Him with all my faith to give me the courage and the tools to make a difference. At that moment I became aware of my responsibility as a human being, and I committed myself to improving humanity. I didn't mind being rich or poor; my mission was simply to help others.

With much sacrifice I graduated from college. My English was not fluent, and I had a hard time communicating orally and in writing, but I worked hard and graduated with honors. My mom was afraid to let me go off to college; it was a world and a system she didn't know. "We don't know anyone there, we don't have money for emergencies and you have never lived on your own. You have scholarships here and don't need to go". In high school I won several scholarships to local colleges, but Occidental College in Los Angeles (where President Obama attended) interested me more because it was the most prestigious. It was also completely free for me because of my academic efforts and personal story.

While thousands of mothers longed to send their children to college, it took a whole mission for us to convince mine, and yet, one day before leaving for college, she wept in hope that I would change my mind. I stayed strong in my decision to leave even though I wanted to stay because I was more afraid of change than my mom was. That night I asked my dad to help me convince her. I knew my dad would help me because he experienced firsthand not being able to make it past elementary. He was expected to work, even though he was one of the brightest in class. At my age it would have been very easy to give up, but thanks to my personal commitment (meaning I voluntarily took on and fulfilled obligations to further my development regardless of resources and/or family support), I started a career in which I stood out professionally.

As expected, given my family's traditional upbringing, I came back home after my graduation, started a relationship, and got married. Apart from giving birth to a talented child, there was nothing extraordinary about my personal life. I felt like I was not keeping the word of that little girl who was committed to overcoming herself. I was surrounded by unmet expectations.

In the last custody court I had with my son's father, I confirmed that my intuition does not lie. During my courtship and marriage, I always felt there were secrets. I lived in anguish and was tired of having to ignore my ex-husband's behavior to avoid fighting. But one great day I decided to take up my life again because I had spent most of my energy in insecurities and anxieties instead of growing as a person and as a couple.

My divorce was very difficult. However, I felt liberated, and although I hit bottom, losing my job and my car and nearly losing my house, I never lost my faith. It is important to reiterate that on several occasions I survived weeks with only one dollar in my pocket. My son at this time was about six years old, and although he did not understand what was happening, he cried every night for his father. The first night that our electricity was cut for lack of payment I was the one who cried because, for the first time, like my son, I felt powerless and alone.

Rarely did I tell my family and friends what was happening to me. In fact, when I shared my challenges, I usually did so when I had already found the solution on my own. Day after day, I came out of one difficulty and quickly entered another. Sounds familiar? During this stage in my life, for the first time, I understood that it was very expensive to be poor and I needed to help myself in order to be able to help others.

Focus on Building Your Passion First

The day I decided to change both my personal and my professional lives, the energy of my circle changed, and in just three years I met my lifetime long-term goals. First, I focused on giving greater results at my job. I earned a promotion and much better pay. I shared my method with others, and we created an efficient team. My talent began to be recognized, and companies started searching me out.

During my career as a recruitment manager, I improved my methodology and began to implement it by focusing on what I was most passionate about: helping people who had potential but were stuck in survival jobs. The method worked! Each person who followed my plan and got a better job and better pay was like a trophy to me. Their gratitude filled me with satisfaction. Similarly, the managers who had vacant positions were very pleased because my team had not only reduced the time it took to find candidates but located candidates with a high professional standard, many of whom were already company employees but no one had ever paid attention to.

I finally felt that I was living the mission of my life. One of my favorite jobs was working for a supermarket based in the South Bay area of California, focused on the Mexican and Latino market. This company's culture of self-improvement inspired me to think of solutions. Although I didn't know how, I felt able to one day automate an individualized growth plan to guide so many talented and hardworking people who wanted to improve professionally but had no idea how to do it.

I tested this methodology with several companies and saw amazing results. People were staying and growing and companies were performing much better (I won't bore you with measurable quantitative results). One of the things I loved most about my role was having the opportunity to listen to so many people during one of the most frightening activities — a job interview. I think I have interviewed a little more than twenty-five thousand people, all for different positions (from cleaning staff to executives), from sectors with different professional profiles, personalities, perspectives, and the like.

At first, I wanted to find jobs for everyone who applied. My first week as a recruiting manager, a man with a disability to speak and walk demanded to be assisted. Everyone in the office seemed to know him, but they didn't make any comment and called me instead. It was my opportunity to demonstrate how to "handle these situations," so I went out to see him, and at that moment my heart broke. I invited him to my office, and he took me by surprise. I let him explain to me with difficulty, "Miss, every week I come to the store to ask for a job, and the manager tells me there are no vacancies. But I see they continue to hire people. I know they shouldn't discriminate against me, and I need the job to help Mom. My dad died, and we can't afford to pay the rent. I know I can put food in bags and clean the bathrooms." He assured me. I swear that I wanted to give him a hug and, of course, the job, however, I was new and had no influence to change the list of profiles required for each position. At that moment my responsibility was to face the situation. First of all, I apologized because no one had taken the time to explain that for every position within the store the profile of the "most suitable" employee required certain skills. I showed him the minimum requirements, and he told me that seven of the ten he did not meet. He thanked me and left disappointed.

Those days were very difficult. We had so much work that we usually didn't have time left over to follow up on situations like that. But I took the time that night, and I sent him a letter reiterating our conversation and included a list of resources and a list of positions I knew he would perform very well. A few weeks later, I received a letter from him thanking me because he had finally found a job.

Sadly, the reality is very different for most people seeking work or a promotion because very few people take the time to guide and help them, perpetuating a vicious circle of inefficiency and loss of talent—like John, the team member that ignited my decision to risk it all and dedicate my life to building something that would help people like him, not just in that company but around the world. I met him because he had applied for an executive position that he clearly didn't fit the profile for. Several in the office mocked him because they didn't understand why this guy, who was a cashier at one of our stores, thought he should apply for that position. As part of my professional ethics, I decided to give him an appointment and to explain why he would not be called for an interview. On the day of our meeting, he arrived very early wearing a professional suit. Before taking him to my office, I decided to present him to all my staff, making sure I told everyone who John was and what his accomplishments so far had been.

Annoyed, once in my office, John asked me, "Why do you say so many good things about me if out of the seventeen times I have applied for a better position within the company, I have been denied for them all? I am twenty-six years old, and ten of those years I have dedicated to this company. I have a university degree in human resources, and I graduated with honors. I don't understand why you don't give me the opportunity."

When John left, I called my team together and asked them to explain why he had not been given the opportunity, but no one had an objective answer. That day, I decided to implement a new process — to help someone understand why he or she was not given the job they applied for and to give feedback to every internal candidate so they could meet the requirements and be promoted at the next opportunity.

And that's how John worked on his plan, and within several weeks, he started as part of my team — at last! John was very dedicated and gave a lot to our department, but one day at a one-on-one meeting, he told me he was struggling with stage-3 cancer. I did my best to support him with this secret (because he didn't want to be treated with pity) until we couldn't hide it anymore. Team members began to notice changes because he was in radiation, and apart from feeling weak, his skin color was too pale. Months later he died. At his funeral, his mother embraced me with much affection and shared that her son died fulfilled because someone had finally believed in him. It was his desire to work for corporate, in an office, exercising what he had studied. My tears flowed, and I told her that working with her son had changed my life forever and that his story would not pass in vain.

My commitment to the growth of others grew with every story I heard of the rejection, of talented people who had so much to contribute but never had a mentor, a guide to follow, or simply transparency from management to understand their talent decisions. That's why I wagered and gambled on a career that has cost me so much to get, to create a company that will give results to thousands of people lost in unsuitable jobs—jobs that don't fill their pockets or their souls.

Like John, I often was met with wrongdoing, hatred, and cruelty too. I have so many stories to tell but I'll share one that I've seen happen to other minority women in positions of influence. An Anglo man who was my senior at this same company, during a meeting, screamed at me and pointed into my face. When I asked administration to look into it, I was told to "grow a thicker skin." What that really meant was that only some of us are expected to take that kind of treatment or to "grow thicker skins." Every large company I saw was filled and fueled by conscious and unconscious inequities, and I felt it, both as a Mexican American employee myself and as an expert in talent management.

I knew I had to drive the kind of cultural and intellectual shift required to make progress, but I couldn't impact wide-scale change, especially as I was fighting the very same issues myself. I would have to do something different. So instead of focusing on the inequities, unfairness, etc. I began thinking of potential solutions, trying new ways, researching what was already out there. And, without any background in it, I realized it would have to be technology because it allows for solutions to scale out globally. Not to mention technology facilitates companies' revenue growth because it helps out a greater number of people. The more people that use the product or service the greater revenue one makes. So I prepared and focused my career in driving and delivering technical implementations and integrations. I spent endless hours testing ideas and methods. I realized the solution would need to be very transparent and show people what it looks like from a 360-degree perspective. If there is a promotion opportunity, there can be no doubt about what's next and what someone must do to qualify. Clients would have to be shown the tactical and practical profitability through data, thereby taking away bias. The numbers would make it clear which candidates were ready. People's lives could change. Generational poverty disproportionately impacting people of color — particularly Latinos of Mexican descent — could change.

Decide on a Goal and Make a Plan

My last experience working for a grocery store turned my passion into a solid life mission. Again, I have never applied to a job; they have usually looked for me. In this case, it was no different. I was already focused on starting my StartUp (a new company) when I was called by executives of this supermarket and presented the opportunity to manage the talent area. I decided to take the challenge because, despite being a company with more than $6 billion in sales and almost 17,000 employees, they did not have the right structure in talent acquisition, including recruitment and personnel strategy, and that motivated me to implement my method and validate my hypothesis, this time with more diverse personnel.

This is where I understood that although Latinos, specifically Mexicans, are the majority in lower-paying jobs in the United States, poverty and lack of professional development marginalizes, regardless of culture or skin color. Shortly after my start we implemented a new process of interviewing and promoting as well as improved advisory systems, electronic applications, and much more, giving results never seen before.

My team confessed to me that when I started, they thought I was a little crazy since the plan I presented was too aggressive and not very credible because they had never done or seen that kind of work done before. Over time though, together we proved the opposite. Each of them grew, improved, and even earned a better salary. Some people consider it luck, but achieving something big takes focus, a plan, and most of all, action.

The greatest satisfaction for me was to see how they fulfilled challenges on their own that they never imagined. That motivated me to test this methodology on myself and fulfill a dream I had growing up but that I saw as unreachable—to produce my own album.

Remember I shared that we traveled in a bus to the United States and the van broke down? In that bus, a man with a guitar in his hand brightened our lives, delighting us with songs from the golden age. I don't even know how it happened, but suddenly, I became the singer of the trip. I think I sang the same song, Joan Sebastian's "El precio," several times because people wanted more, and as I was very young, I hardly knew any songs. I went from imitating artists of the moment like Trevi, Selena, and Alicia de Límite to falling in love with voices rancheras like Aida Cuevas and even Linda Ronstadt (with her CD *Canciones a mi Padre*). My uncles, who already knew I liked to sing, encouraged me when we had a party in the family, and more so when the music was live.

Although with time I have developed technique and experience singing, I think I compose much better. Like everyone else in show business, I have received unpleasant mockeries and comments, but I don't get overwhelmed. I sing and compose because I enjoy it. As a child I always dreamed of delighting audiences with my music. What better way to prove that when you have a talent, a vision that goes hand in hand with your passion, a plan, and a network of people in the right environment, you can do anything.

After being a finalist for a national Mariachi competition, I knew I had talent. It was then that I began to see myself as a singer, a professional singer, so I started performing and charging, and I began to save all that "extra" money. Eventually I saved enough to record an album with all original content, a music video, presented my album at a private party for family and friends, performed at big festivals, opened for major artists like Banda el Limón, Los Tigres del Norte, and Luis Coronel, and wrote songs and corridos for other local artists. I achieved all of this in just one year of focus and dedication— all the while developing the idea of my company, keeping my job as part of the executive team of a supermarket chain, and being a single mom.

Although I have reduced my presentations and recordings to focus my energy on being a better entrepreneur, I have the intuition that one day my two passions will be the joy of humanity. Therefore, little by little I continue to do what fills my soul and intentionally share it with my community and followers on social media to hopefully inspire cultural and professional empowerment. This kind of passion and messaging is also represented in my music, such as one of my favorite songs I've composed called "Llora Mi Cuerpo" ("My Body Cries"). Martha Soledad is my artist name.

But "how did I get to doing so much," as many frequently ask? Well, I am one of those extremely positive, can-do-anything, pick-up-fast-if-you-fall kind of people who sometimes is disliked by those who can't see the light at the end of the tunnel. My younger sister, I think, was the first one to share a reality that I had a hard time assimilating. I do not consider myself extraordinary; in fact, like everyone else I have thousands of moments of doubt and, of course, defects. But I think the difference is that I only like to share (and more so in social networks) the positive aspects of my life. This has resulted in admiration but has also brought a little negative energy into my circle.

Take Care of Your Energy and Address Your Fears

Three years ago, I won a brand-new, super-giant RAM truck at a business conference. The weekend before I'd had a revelation. It was a Sunday, and I was sad because I had negotiated with the car dealership to terminate my car contract since I couldn't afford to continue paying the fee. I was just starting my job and had no idea how I was going to get there. I remember going out into the street, and as I finished cleaning the inside of the car, I closed the door and stood behind the trunk. I saw its license plates for the last time and thought of everything this car had been through with me. I asked God to give me a car so I could take my son to school and start my job safely. At that moment, I kind of wanted to laugh at myself, but strangely enough, I convinced myself that winning a car was possible. It was a moment of great faith and immense humbleness as I gave thanks for giving me the experience of falling and the hope of getting up.

The next day I arrived at the conference in Texas. I remember the sponsors had a lot of raffles all over the exhibit room, but since I didn't have business cards yet, I couldn't participate. However, I felt like I was going to win something. The Chrysler Company announced at the end of the conference it would raffle the truck. I immediately knew it was for me. With the little I had in the bank, I gambled my luck and bought a ticket. Approximately fifteen hundred people were present, and it was my name that was called. I won the big prize! I got on the stage, was photographed, and then I ran to call my mom.

When I got home, my mom told me that not everyone was happy for my good luck; when she told her friends what had happened to me, they reacted with envy. I didn't know what envy was. In fact, when I interviewed Latinos and asked them why they left their last job, most of the answers were "Because they were envious of me." I discarded such a comment and said to myself, *Another one with the same story.* This time I understood because my sister commented to me, "Ay, Martha, if I, who am your sister have felt envy towards you, imagine those who do not know you or love you." (At that moment my life had a pause.) She explained to me that although she felt happy about my achievements, she often wondered "Why Martha and not me?"

It was then I understood that envy was the desire to have what another person has and that this desire, this thought that goes through our minds without realizing it, is what generates the separation of "luck" and guilt towards the other person for our apparent "bad luck." At that moment I understood we all have this weakness, but very few of us know how to recognize it, much less unplug it. My sister, who is mature and wise, opened my eyes. Personally, I decided to become aware of this feeling, to not affect the energy of others when my need and ego demands the abundance of others, and to not let this feeling in other people affect the chance of success in me. It is a constant struggle, but it is worth it because it has liberated my dreamy spirit from the bad energies of either my own feelings or the feelings of others. On this journey, I learned that when you are committed to achieving something, no matter how small, there is no time to be overwhelmed by the accomplishments of others, no matter how great they may be. It was clear that living free of envy and bad energy was my choice. What I did not know was how to live free from fear.

The last time I took my son to the zoo, I realized something serious was happening to me. As usual, we finished our visit and returned to the front of the park in a gondola. We both loved it. But this day it was different. As I sat on the gondola, I felt a bit of anxiety. I grabbed on to my son, and it went away until little by little my feet stopped feeling the ground. Then I awoke a fear I had never felt. In seconds, I thought to scream so that they returned to us, because my mind was sure we were going to fall. But I immediately started focusing on my son and rationalizing we were in a safe place; plus, he was having fun.

A few seconds later I picked up my phone and began reading articles on recommendations for people with anxiety and panic problems. I learned to do three things: 1) help my mind get back to normal by eating, drinking, or touching something (I didn't have food with me, so I hugged my son and took him by the hand); 2) take a deep breath and think about pleasant things, like a favorite song; and 3) accept that what was happening to me. Though it's not common, it is normal for people in situations like mine—several things had happened to me that usually don't happen all at the same time: the death of a loved one, losing a job, and divorce, all in two years.

Focus on Your Plan and Make Progress Everyday—No Excuses

At that time, I got recruited for a nonprofit organization that brought me in to develop a new program preparing unemployed people to get a job. Although I loved my job, it was depressing. Companies looking for talent expected a certain type of candidate, and the people looking for work lived in conditions of great need and, unfortunately, did not meet the requirements of available jobs. Our program was effective, but the impact was minimal. I felt desperate because I knew I could do more, but the organization had a slightly more relaxed culture. By this time, I already had in mind the idea of my business (and even knew what I was going to call it: madeBOS, "made by own self").

A year after working there, my ex-boss (from that supermarket in the South Bay area) called me and asked me to consider a position on the executive team of a large, reputable company. The salary was more than double what I was earning at the not-for-profit, but I had to move to the valley. It was a very important decision because it was the opportunity to save money and finally develop the idea of my company. The only thing that held me was fear because I had no family in this new city. After careful evaluation, I decided to move. It was a step in the right direction to continue my long-term plan of building madeBOS.

Being alone with my son in a new community was incredibly difficult. My son cried every day at school; I realized some of his classmates were bullying him. At work, things were incredibly difficult because it was a conservative culture, and the decisions were only accepted from the men who had been working there for decades. I got sick, and I suffered from depression, anxiety, and a lot of loneliness. However, every time I felt I was falling in the dark, I got up quickly because I knew I had a purpose in this life. Solving problems or facing adversity was nothing new to me. I knew I could do it. My mind got used to seeing problems as learning experiences and quickly thinking creatively about solutions.

My energy soon influenced others at my job, and they began to support my vision. Over time I told them about my plan to impact the world, and even my boss began to support me. I invested my savings in developing my idea, madeBOS, turned my vacation into conferences, and got education into the startup environment. I learned to ask for help, to develop a network of resources, and even to diversify my income (singing, giving leadership classes, consulting, etc.). I fell in love with the idea of changing lives at scale, and that empowered me to visualize the future—a beautiful, more equitable future and to not give up, no matter the circumstances or the challenges presented. Let's be real—life happens, and as you can already tell, life has definitely happened to me, but I don't focus on that. I accept that as part of life, and focus on what can be, when it can be, and what I need to do to make it happen.

Now I'm back at home and, with family, creating what will someday be a big company. Let's be clear. I'm not the smartest, but I'm a very brave coward who doesn't let the fear she feels every day define how much can be achieved.

Find Those Who Push You But Also Celebrate You

My practice of knocking on doors and selling nopales when I was a kid worked. Of course, I still haven't fulfilled my dream of selling nopales door to door in my beautiful town of Chavinda (hahaha), but I did have success when I sold office supplies door to door all over the Bay Area. When I first started as a sales representative, my boss personally gave me my first training because, from the beginning, she saw my desire to excel. Unfortunately, no other sales representatives took the time to get to know me; they even ignored my lunch invitations, which, usually, the right thing to do when a new employee was hired was to have lunch with them. Those who did take me into account and were supportive of me were those who worked in administration, customer service, and deliveries, since most of them were Latino and African American. They told me they were proud to see a young Latina in sales making it happen, so they were all in with me.

I was afraid to fail because my job depended on my ability to sell; in fact, I was so terrified that I creatively found ways to sell more. Therefore, my first month, and most of the subsequent months, I was at 300–400 percent of my sales goal and striving to win the challenges with bonus incentives. With these kinds of results, I won the team and gradually started training new employees by sharing my strategies. I was quickly promoted to new and better paid positions.

Knocking on doors and being rejected thousands of times was a great foundation in my professional development because I learned to 1) be creative in seeking alternatives to get a yes, 2) create a specific plan to not give up, 3) focus energies on objective factors, and finally, 4) surround myself with people who believe in my vision and are inspired by my solution proposals. It's also interesting that in almost every position I've held, the team at first didn't believe in me or my ability to deliver something productive and impacting. I don't seem to represent what they usually recognize as "successful" or "having potential" — just like the thousands of people I've interviewed who have remained trapped in service or blue-collar positions. This problem of conscious and unconscious bias and prejudice is not only seen in novels where the rich are whites who live in prosperous cities and the poor are "prietitos de provincia" (people of color from provinces) but is a real problem I have to live every day. Moreover, meeting people who are constantly thinking about solutions and ideas that generate change and sometimes new expectations does not thrill people who usually sit in a position and exercise the minimum to keep it. I have had to tolerate harassment, screams, threats, and even extortion from people who are uncomfortable with my energy and confidence in myself and my team.

All these experiences have not been in vain. For the first time, I signed my own job offer as chief executive officer of madeBOS. Formalizing my relationship with my company as founder and executive director was a great achievement. I'm not saying I'm at the top; on the contrary, I'm in the most difficult and culminating position, once again facing several challenges—including the number one challenge any startup in the early stage has, which is access to capital. American companies that excel are usually founded by Anglos who have strong social capital—that is, between family and friends, they can raise thousands of dollars to develop their ideas and create their products and solutions. Moreover, this social capital includes connections within the venture capital world. Therefore, when I studied this environment and learned that traditionally less than 1 percent of investments goes to companies founded by Latinos (and for those by Latina women, the number is even lower), I needed to find funding alternatives.

In addition, the journey, although exciting, also over time became disappointing. I had heard people say this, but I didn't understand what it meant until it happened to me. At the beginning, everybody loved my business idea. People made promises. My network wanted me to succeed, but when I followed up, nothing happened. I can't tell you how many times I was so deeply disappointed. When it comes down to it, no one's going to move the finger to make anything significant happen for you unless they benefit personally—that's reality. I remember one day I woke up, and I thought, "Wow. What if this is not the right idea? Maybe I should be building something else. What have I done, dragging my team with me?"

And that was when everything changed. Because that bit of ego about me was gone—that sense of thinking I could not get venture capitalists to invest in my idea. The work became the focus, and eventually, we found our funding tribe.

My team and I raised funds in a crowdfunding campaign, a new alternative to the investment process that gives anyone, regardless of social status, the opportunity to invest in startups. When we launched the campaign, I immediately thought my family and friends were going to invest. But the first day of campaigning passed, then the first week, and it didn't happen. Only those who understood the investment ecosystem immediately invested in madeBOS. As part of my commitment to democratizing opportunities, I decided to use the equity crowdfunding method through the Republic.co platform regulated by the Security Employment Commission (SEC), which oversees all investments, and to share future profits with people who recognize the potential of madeBOS and who will have the opportunity to be investors. However, it was not easy; we learned that the community does not understand this concept and we have to invest much more energy in educating, educating, and further educating our community.

With only twenty-five days left of the investment campaign, I decided to tell part of my story to my social media followers and reiterate that, just like me, they also had a responsibility to fulfill. We need to change the narrative, and instead of just being helpful, we also need to be creative and enterprising. Our commitment must be more than the monetary incentive, although it is also very necessary to equalize our capitalist culture and include and recognize the contribution of all types of people regardless of gender, sex, skin color, nationality, and the like. It is necessary to challenge and conquer our behaviors and tendencies to make ourselves small.

We need to end our disbelief in achieving greatness. We must support leaders who are willing to contribute but are born with social and financial disadvantages because it is very likely they will bring solutions to the world's most difficult problems.

The messaging worked. We raised 217 percent of our goal (the majority by first-time Latino investors), used that money to create an MVP (minimum valuable product), and we ran a pilot. The moment I truly knew we were on the right track was when I spoke to one of our participants who reminded me of that young man who had passed away. He said to me, "Every time I'm in front of a computer and looking for a job, I see so many job listings, and it's overwhelming. That's not the worst part. The worst is that I don't feel I'm good enough for anything I see. The first time using madeBOS, I felt for the first time I was a good fit for three careers (not even just "jobs"), and I learned how to actually get there. No one has ever told me how to get to a job like that."

I felt so empowered, knowing that we were making a real difference in people's lives, and not just for "my people" — Latinos and Latinas. madeBOS is made for all people, for anyone who has ever struggled to be seen and valued, and in this country, this often means all black and brown people, immigrants and their children, and rural Americans, who, by the way, often only have access to low-end jobs at corporate big box stores. Some people have told me, "Your app is only for Latinos." That comment tells me so much about their perspectives — they are unwilling to admit and see the billions of people living in generational poverty, and what that hopelessness means for our entire world.

Shortly after conducting our pilot, I applied to Camelback Ventures. Coming from Silicon Valley, I had been in other programs, shadowed other people, been interviewed. An hour before my Camelback interview, I prepared to "do my hair" — literally, undo my curls, flatten them, as I was used to doing for every other funder meeting. But something stopped me. I wondered, Can I really just be myself? And so I was. My co-founder at the time sat with me during my interview, off-camera, to support me. After I finished, he said, "Wow. There's no doubt you'll get it." I was surprised and asked why he thought so. "Because of the synergy. There's a common goal. This is what you've been looking for. They get it. They see you."

I've knocked on doors, hustled, shared my message, demonstrating my expertise. But in the Silicon Valley, that's the base of what's expected. But what Camelback saw in me was that I wasn't everybody.

They saw the distance I had traveled, what I had had to overcome, way beyond any other individuals in the traditional funding route. When he said, "They see you," I felt for the first time that it was me, all of me, that was valued.

Have a Higher Purpose Focused on Something Bigger

Today, when times get difficult, I think of those who *need* to see me successful—my own people, Mexican Americans. In this nation alone, in the minority population overall, the largest ethnic minority are of Hispanic and Latino descent— 52 million people. Latinos drive that number, and over 60 percent of Latinx immigrants come from Mexico. And the majority of those come from my home-state, Michoacán. This was a result of that state's partnership with the US starting in the 1940s, the Bracero Program—recruitment for agricultural labor.

When I first looked at these numbers, I felt so empowered. I felt this intense responsibility, and that gave me strength. I had the numbers of the people behind me who had been hiding, who have been hidden, those who have been working day in and day out, in poverty. People whose talents have been ignored, because their cheap labor was deemed more valuable. My people have been kept in this cycle in America for over seventy years, with anyone who pushed back threatened, deported, or silenced.

I learned that Mexico is *third in the world* in producing software engineers, though I had never heard of it before. But guess what? Very few are in leadership or entrepreneurial positions. For the most part, they are in a maquiladora role (i.e., subcontractors, working for international development shops, and mostly for other United States companies and often in low level coding work).

And what is my outcome for madeBOS? It's unlocking potential. Regardless of where you're at in your career or in the world, we want to unlock your potential and empower you to grow into the work and life that you want and deserve. I felt empowered again. I realized I could use my power with my organization to not just create a mission-driven product but could implement my passion and identity in my own practices by being intentional about who will continue to build our software. So, I booked tickets and rented an office in Guadalajara, Jalisco, Mexico. I had interviews lined up with local organizations and successfully partnered with two value-aligned entrepreneurs to continue our software development and talent search.

I have taken this opportunity very seriously to implement what I have learned in my trajectory in the development of human talent and leadership. Inventing a new methodology with a global potential does not happen every day, so I have bet on myself and on madeBOS. At first, my mom and my sisters didn't understand much of this, but when they saw I left my job, they understood it was serious and even more so when they witnessed the mentors, the team, and the prestigious law firm and bank supporting the company.

Three years ago I didn't have the social capital to create a company, but I have invested all of myself— long hours, weekends, savings, and so on—plus my experience managing various teams and billion-dollar budgets, implementing, configuring, and integrating more than fifteen technological systems and restructuring processes and changing behaviors to ensure objectivity in the selection of talent. I know my team can, and I know that I can; therefore, we are on the right track, and every day we advance in our plan. There is always an alternative to achieve what everyone in this world has the opportunity to win, and madeBOS is an example of that. He who does not risk does not win. So, the question is, *would you like to buy nopales?*

Thank you very much for giving me this opportunity to share with you my story "From nopalera to CEO." The hustle continues — we are in this together.

CHAPTER 2

ESTELA LOPEZ

Living Compass Community Wellness Advocate
and Entrepreneur

**Trials are not meant to destroy us,
but to equip us for our purpose.**

Sometimes we give up at the first setback, without knowing that our struggles are part of the journey that will lead to success. Do not be afraid of failure or adversity because each mistake teaches us a lesson. We should get out of our comfort zone and try as many times as we need to and never give up on our dreams. Often, we will need to change the plan and be willing to adapt according to the circumstances but never change the goal. Do not worry too much about the naysayers, those who are not failing are not even trying either.

I am originally from Guadalajara, Mexico. The city of Guadalajara is beautiful and well known for mariachi music and Tequila. I never would have thought that one day I was going to leave my country. I come from a big family of five brothers and three sisters. I am number five from the oldest to the youngest. Coming from a large family is not something negative as many believe. I think it is great blessing because you will always have a faithful friend in each of them.

My father immigrated to the US seeking a better quality of life for his family. He would come back home every year in December during the holidays. He did it for fifteen long years. Those were the hardest years for our family. My father's absence caused me pain and sadness. My dad missed too many of our birthday celebrations and the joy of watching his kids grow. My mom had to struggle living as if she was a single mom, trying to raise eight kids by herself. She cried in silence many nights, probably because she was tired and overwhelmed most of the time. That experience of growing up without my father made me mature quickly. It developed my emotional intelligence, pushed me to be very independent, and to work hard for the things I wanted. I genuinely believe that adversity builds character and makes us stronger.

One day, my mom courageously made the decision to reunite us with our dad. I was sixteen years old when we came to this country, undocumented, along with my family. That was the scariest moment of my life, but I did not have any other choice but to be strong. I remember we walked for days without eating or drinking water, and I almost drowned crossing the US border at the Rio Grande. I am a doer and an achiever, and since that near-death experience, I promised myself I was going to learn how to swim—and I did eventually. Resilience is a necessary virtue for times of hardships, and every time we overcome adversities, we gain confidence in ourselves.

Once we settled down in our new home in the Chicago area, my parents registered my younger siblings in school, and I was asked to work to support the family instead of attending school. I worked full time in a cafeteria, and then after coming home, I studied English using a home-study course called "Ingles sin Barreras" (English without Borders); I had always considered myself autodidactic. When there is a will, there is a way; the rest is just excuses. Ignorance is a choice, especially nowadays that we have full access to information through the internet. Many people use YouTube for entertainment, when one can use it to learn new skills or for personal development.

At first, I did not like the fact that I was not given the opportunity to attend school like my younger siblings. However, the experience of working at a young age taught me to have courage and self-determination, to go out there and work it out until I find the opportunities I wanted in life. Even though I was living with my parents, my money had a purpose. Without realizing it, I lived from an envelope-system budget. Since I didn't have access to credit cards or have a bank account, I only used cash. My money was primarily to pay bills, to buy groceries, and to save to buy a used car. Whenever the envelope was empty, then it was time to stop spending. Simple as that! I couldn't do anything else until the next paycheck arrived, because it is not how much money you make but how much you spend. It is easy to get caught up in the spending mode or fall into trends. For example, I never bought brand new cars or replaced my cell phone for the latest version just because everyone else was doing it.

At age nineteen I got pregnant. Knowing things were going to be difficult for me, I decided to take my

GED test. I knew education was very important, not only as personal growth but to open in my life doors of new opportunities. Knowledge is power and is the only one thing nobody can take from you.

After giving birth to my first child, I went to work for a car insurance agency, nine hours a day, six days a week, which was the most stressful job I ever had. Just thinking of my job would give me anxiety from dealing with car claims and angry customers. However, this job experience taught me excellent soft skills like problem-solving, work ethic, and adaptability. Hard skills such a degree or a certificate can get you hired, but lack of soft skills can get you fired.

Although it was not my dream job, I was willing to learn and go the extra mile, always on time and with a positive attitude. Later, I realized this job was overwhelming for my artistic personality. I do not like fixed schedules; I prefer to work in unstructured situations where I can use my creativity and imagination. I knew then that a job with flexible hours would be a better fit for me. That way I could spend more time with my son. I wanted a meaningful job where I could help people feel good about themselves.

In 2002, I finally became a US citizen, which was a great accomplishment for me. Citizenship offered me full rights and benefits but also responsibilities such as exercising my right to vote. My personal story as immigrant and my struggles have brought me to work for the common good as community organizer. I plead with you to become a citizen if you are eligible. Part of growing up as an insightful adult, is to get involved in the decisions that are made locally in your city. Become a person of influence and make your voice heard by voting. Register to vote and vote early. If we don't vote, we don't count.

The same year, I decided to join the beauty industry to get my cosmetology license. That was the most fulfilling job I ever had. I did it for ten years. I loved the transformation process clients went through, from sometimes feeling depressed to gaining confidence and recovering their self-esteem. Having a person sitting on my chair was a very sacred moment for me and an opportunity to influence and encourage them. Without knowing it, I was already doing some type of coaching. Since then, I discovered I have a passion to help people to become the best version of themselves through goal-setting, personal growth, and behavior modification. Once I healed the wounds from my past, I was able to be an instrument for other people. I believe that we are healed to heal. Thankfully, my pain and trials had a purpose. I became a healer. My faith has played a huge role in my healing process.

Just when I thought I had it all figured it out, my husband, and I bought our first home, a condominium. Sadly, later we found out that condominiums do not appreciate as much as residential homes. We did not have anyone to give us good advice at the time, and that was our first bad financial decision. Because of that reason, I became a licensed real estate agent. Taking advantage of my leadership skills, I wanted to use the knowledge to help people, offering them honest advice and assist them in their home purchases. However, I entered the business at the wrong time. Because of the Great Recession in 2008, people were not buying houses; instead, they were losing their own homes.

In 2012 we moved to Houston, Texas. I had to reinvent myself one more time. My husband, a priest in the Episcopal church, was called to restart a mission that was about to close its doors. We ministered together, where I put into practice my skills of organization, teamwork, and conflict resolution by leading multiple fundraising events and festivals and creating programs for adults, youth, and children. One of the programs I enjoy the most was teaching Folkloric dance because when I dance, I feel so alive. We even offered these classes free for the recreation of the kids and their parents because when we use our gifts and talents to serve the community, it gives us joy and a sense of fulfillment.

I have always dreamed of creating job opportunities for people in my own country. I am convinced of the importance of empowering women by supporting the artisans of Mexico and Latin America. My sister-in-law, and I are proud of our culture and our traditions. Together, we started an online store where we promote the artisans' colorful and unique work with the world in a socially responsible way. At MiTierraArtisanCrafts.com, every purchase has the power to build a sustainable business for our artisans and their families.

Do not let fear stop you from pursuing your dreams. There is nothing "impossible" to achieve, for the word itself says "I'm possible." Embrace your story and the pain that comes with it. Often, our struggles prepare us to live our lives with a purpose.

5 Keys to Success:

1. Decide what you want.

   A student may say, "I don't know what I want." Don't worry too much; life goes by seasons. At this season of your life, choose a career that will suit your personal needs, but also explore ways you can serve others with your career choice. Remember, when we give, we also receive. Don't be afraid of choosing a career. I am thirty-nine years old, yet I recently went back to school to pursue another dream.

2. Associate with successful people.

   Life can be hard and overwhelming at times. We need to make sure we are surrounded by people who have similar goals, people who are relentless workers, people who have big dreams, people who are positive and great motivators. Success is a collaborative process; we cannot make it by ourselves. We all need a tribe as well as accountability. Make sure you find the support and the advice from the right tribe. Keep on looking for it until you find the right one.

3. Plan your work and work your plan.

   You must have a strategy to be able to reach your goals. Planning is the first step to success. How you organize your time will determine your results.

   a) Use an agenda, follow it, and update it each day.

   b) Avoid procrastination: don't put it off; do it now! Don't rest until you do.

   c) Develop the habit of having a to-do list. Tackle the most challenging task, and break down big projects into more manageable tasks.

   d) Do not snooze your alarm clock. Something that has worked for me is to start my day with the five-second rule, which is getting out of bed by counting 5-4-3-2-1. This technique eliminates laziness as well as the doubts and fears that keep you from reaching your goals.

4. Do all things with excellence. Do it until you make it a habit. Be the best you can be at home, school, and work. You will be surprised how the Creator, along with the universe, will start conspiring in your favor to help you get promoted, to reach your goals

by putting the right people on your path and opening doors of new opportunities.

5. Choose to be an adaptable person. Change is inevitable and is the only way to grow. Be open to change. Adaptability is essential to be a valuable leader. It makes you a team player. Allow yourself to make mistakes and learn from them.

Be brave and courageous. You have what it takes within you to reach your goals and to be successful. But it is necessary to change your perspective completely to start seeing failure and difficulties as an opportunity to grow to be able to live your life to the fullest potential.

CHAPTER 3

ANDREA GUENDELMAN

When I was growing up in Chile, people I met for the first time would ask me about my grandfather. They would inevitably recite, "*usted lo ve, lo prueba y se lo lleva.*" This phrase – you see it, you try it, you take it – was the slogan that made the department store my grandfather started famous. He succeeded because of this phrase. It captured his novel business model of selling to people form lower income communities, whom the rest of the marketplace ignored. This phrase also explains my own success and credo. I repeat it as a personal and career mantra.

I repeat "you see it, you try it, you take it" because it reminds me of where I came from. Like many entrepreneurs, my success story took inspiration from my family. My grandfather came from a town in Odessa, Russia, where Jews were impoverished, denied education and basic rights, and persecuted. The city has a dark history of pogroms. At age 9, my grandfather fled first to Argentina with no father and only a third grade education. He had only the tailor trade that he learned from his father in Odessa. He soon moved to Chile, where he started a tailor shop that later became started to extend credit terms to people at a time that credit cards did not exist. The tailor shop became a department store and ultimately one of the largest in Chile.

I say the mantra, "you see it, you try it, you take it," to remind myself not only of my grandfather. It also reminds me not to overlook marginalized communities. My grandfather saw people in these communities who deserved dignity. It was not only a business opportunity, it was also a calling. I bring this same attitude to Wallbreakers, my startup. My co-founder, Isaac Saldana, and I want to connect university students from underrepresented backgrounds to opportunities in the tech sector. Companies cannot afford to overlook these talented young people.

I also say the mantra -- *usted lo ve, lo prueba y se lo lleva*/you see it, you try it, you take it – because it captures an entrepreneurial spirit. I remind myself that I need to see opportunities, I need to try them, and I need to take them. An entrepreneur must embrace experiments and seize chances. This spirit animates Wallbreakers. It is something we also hope to pass on to the talented students we connect to tech companies. These students also need to embrace risk and ambition.

Family Expectations

I did not embrace this spirit initially. My path to becoming an entrepreneur was long and winding. It is important to embrace your family history but also to escape their expectations. My grandfather expected his children to become professionals. So they did. My father studied engineering in Chile and later received a PhD in seismic engineering from Berkeley, where I was born. However, his father died suddenly, and, as the oldest son, he had to hurry back to Chile to take care of the family business.

My father also wanted me to become a professional because that is what his father wanted for him. The thought of becoming an entrepreneur and starting your own business was never discussed. There was an unspoken expectation that my brother, as the the oldest and as a male, would eventually take over the family business. Although I had dreams of getting involved in the family business, I pursued my father's ambition. I thought that if I became a tax lawyer, I could eventually join the business *and* be the professional the family prized.

My father's death and the closing of the business shattered that dream. I still had something to prove though. I pursued and succeeded at his dream of me becoming a professional. I earned a law degree in Chile and then another law degree at Harvard. I practiced as a corporate lawyer at a large international firm, then as a government lawyer. I had "made it."

Even so, I was deeply unsatisfied. I still dreamed of business and of doing something creative. I left the law and started planning large scale conferences and events that dealt with the entrepreneurship and technology communities. My first event was a large music and entrepreneurship festival in Chile, which brought together more than ten thousand attendees, featured Al Gore as a keynote speaker, and raised close to $1 million. In later events

Eventually, I expanded these events to talk about how the tech and startup communities might include more women and people from underrepresented communities. As I had lived in New Mexico, I started to see more and more of the Latino community, realizing that's who I wanted to focus on. I ended up creating a company, just like my grandfather had done, which was very appealing to me.

So I've had a long journey toward becoming an entrepreneur. This journey has been the equivalent of a graduate education. It has taught me that I need to follow a set of principles, which I want to share with you.

Principles

Starting a company has been a cross between a multi-year roller coaster and pursuing graduate degrees in business and psychology at the same time. I've received both thrills and lasting lessons thanks to Wallbreakers.com, a platform that finds, trains, and refers entry-level, underrepresented software engineers from universities across the country (computer science majors) to tech companies, and prior to that, BeVisible.soy, a social media platform that connects LatinX professionals to companies hungry for diverse talent. As an entrepreneur, I have seen amazing growth and suffered near-death experiences. Although the roller-coaster ride continues, I'm working to make sure it is the business that experiences the twists and turns, not my psyche. Accordingly, here are ten lessons I've distilled for myself to make my entrepreneurial journey less of a carnival ride and more of a solid education.

1. Relationship "Fit" Is Crucial

Whether it is hiring employees, locating investors, or finding partners, personal fit matters just as much as a gold-plated resume or dollars and cents. In fact, neither a potential partner with a stellar curriculum vitae or an investor willing to contribute a lot of capital are worth doing a deal with if the relationship is not right. A relationship needs to be built on mutual respect, open lines of communication, and clear accountability. All three items are necessary and reinforce one another. Doing great in two of these areas cannot compensate for problems in the third. Indeed, respect needs to be the foundation on which the house is built.

Culture may make all the difference in determining whether a solid business relationship can grow. Culture may have little to do with a person's ethnic or religious background. Indeed, I've seen potential partners with similar upbringings who have vastly different working styles and built divergent business cultures around them. Some people prefer an environment with mano a mano competition within a team. For others, like me, a team of rivals can quickly devolve into Hunger Games. I find I work best in a more low-key culture that focuses on collaborative problem solving instead of interpersonal competition. I imagine many women are in the same position.

2. Delegation: Agreement and Not Just Expectations

Determining what tasks to delegate and to whom is one of the hardest challenges I have faced as an entrepreneur. In the beginning, when the team is small (just a handful or even one person), everyone may do everything. But as the team grows, this approach no longer works. It has been difficult to let go of duties, but I've learned I cannot do everything, and I must leverage the talents of others.

In delegating responsibility, it is important to return to three fundamentals of a good business relationship: mutual respect, open communication, and clear accountability. Each member of a team needs to take ownership. I've learned an important lesson from Steve Chandler about the distinction between expectations and agreement. I've found it is important to have high expectations of a team member (and myself), but that is not enough. These expectations need to be communicated and agreed to. Ideally, they are formed collaboratively rather than set by edict. Agreement, not just expectations, is vital to avoid disappointment and focus the team relentlessly on problems.

3. Self-Reliance

Some things, however, cannot be delegated. One of the hardest lessons I've learned is that decisions on certain things cannot be delegated even to key investors without a founder surrendering her role and becoming an employee. Ultimate ownership of business model and financial decisions needs to rest with the first owner of the company—me. An entrepreneur cannot pick and choose which parts of the business to focus on based on where her or his passions lie. Everything needs to work. Starting a business will quickly expose an entrepreneur's weaknesses. That means avoiding the thorniest problems and parts of a business can be a recipe for disaster. When a core part of the business needs attention, an entrepreneur needs to roll up her sleeves and get to work—learning new skills if need be.

4. Back to Basics: Clients First

Solving the problems and putting out the daily brushfires of a business can drive an entrepreneur to distraction. It has been important for me to keep my North Star: what serves clients. What will help

BeVisible's thousands of LatinX members connect with career and educational opportunities and each other? What will help companies find diverse talent and transform their workplaces and the American workforce? This is not only important for my business, it is important for me as a person. Finding answers to these questions was what drove me to the irrational act of starting a business. Focusing on these questions also keeps me grounded—mentally and spiritually. Deepak Chopra, not usually thought of as a business consultant, put it this way.

5. Boundless and Boundaries

BeVisible's overarching mission isn't the only thing I need to keep me grounded. People who meet me often remark on my contagious energy. But that energy is not boundless. I've found I need to put some boundaries on my energy—to put one foot in front of another—to keep BeVisible's growth on track. Again, what works for the business is also good for the soul. I've learned I need to work hard each day but respect my personal time: my time for family and friends and my time for me. I need to recharge every day or BeVisible suffers as a business, and I suffer as the person at its core. I have learned I need to keep seeking joy and practice gratitude.

6. Combating Disbelief

Even more than career setbacks, the times I've found myself most dispirited is when I've encountered the quiet corrosiveness of that feeling the people around me don't believe in me. Lack of belief feels worse than conflict or an insult. There isn't a quick visceral way to respond. When you are emotionally punched, you can punch back. When others don't have confidence in you, there isn't an easy comeback.

I don't think I'm alone. Women and minorities face this situation again and again in the workplace. And our identities leave us with a truly horrible set of alternatives: Is it us, or is it our gender, our race, our orientation, or something else?

But there is good news. No matter who you are there are lots of things you can do to make sure that a lack of confidence from others doesn't affect your own self-confidence. I've learned several life hacks that have helped me:

a) Surround yourself. To persevere when others lack faith in you, the essential step is to change the people who surround you. To change the plot and mood, you may need to change the cast of the play. Surround yourself with your people — not just people who love you but also people who believe in your talents and your future. Love isn't enough. We all have relatives who are full of love, but they are also quick to feel sorry for you or, even worse, bring you down. Everyone needs a team behind them that overflows with love and respect.

b) Turn the switch. You can also use the disrespect of others as a crucial fuel for motivation. "I'll show them" can be your mantra. It doesn't have to be tinged with bitterness. After all, the best revenge is a life well lived.

7. Combating Fear

Like all entrepreneurs, I have a strange relationship with fear. It used to be a stranger. Then it was an enemy. Now I consider fear to be a frenemy.

I began my journey as an entrepreneur without a notion of fear. You might call it irresponsible or arrogant. I did not know there was a limit, and I thought I was capable of anything. I was passionate to solve a problem: connecting LatinX, women, and other diverse individuals to companies hungry for talent. My passion made me feel I could overcome any obstacle or limitation. It was the opposite mentality from my training as a lawyer. Instead of seeing risk, I only saw opportunity.

The old saying about marriage applies to entrepreneurship too: "It's good that we don't have any clue how difficult the road will be, or we'd never get started." But for me, the startup road became increasingly difficult and littered with obstacles: making sales, keeping team members motivated, finding capital, continuously adjusting the business model, sizing up competition, burning through limited cash. At some point, as months turned to years, my cerebral circuit switched from invulnerability to fear: *maybe this idea wouldn't work, maybe I didn't have the horsepower, maybe I didn't have the luck.*

I decided to keep running. And thank the Lord, I did. I'm still on the marathon. I found two lessons keep me running.

First, it's about digging deeper—not just for me but for my idea and my ideals. I meet young millennials every day struggling to crack into the major leagues of the innovation ecosystem. I hear the challenges they've overcome: limited family resources, first in the family to go to college, taking care of sick parents, siblings, or kids. My fears seem minuscule in comparison. These millennials are an inspiration.

They don't believe the stereotypes the media has stuck on their generation.

Second, it's about enjoying the run, getting into the flow. Fear has a purpose and a place, but it needs to stay in its place. Like physical pain, fear can remind us of real problems that need to be dealt with. But that is the sum and limit of the benefit of fear. If you give it too much respect, it takes over.

Here are some of the steps I take to keep fear under control:

1. Note it: When I start feeling afraid in running my business, I've found it is important not to ignore the feeling, otherwise it can come back in unexpected ways. So I just note to myself, "Ok, I'm having this feeling." Then I ask myself why I am having it.
2. Concrete plan: Once I identify what is bothering me, I break it into a series of concrete problems I need to solve. For example, if I am having trouble making a sale, I rethink customer needs, come up with an action plan of specific short-, medium-, and long-term steps I need to take to meet those needs, and then execute.
3. Adrenalize: Once I start executing, I take a break and find a way to exercise hard.

Accelerating heart rate, surging adrenaline, and cascading sweat all break one mental loop and get me on a much better one.

4. Staying present: After the workout, it is important to keep my mind present. While working, I focus on the action list. But I also need to stay balanced and within boundaries. When I'm not working, I recharge my batteries with my family and friends. I try to stay present in every conversation with them. It is a matter of practice, not mastery — sometimes I fall off the wagon, and fear of the past or the future creeps in. But in the present, there is no fear. There is only passion and love.

5. How do you know how much to trust? Trust is a precious resource in business. Without it, businesses can't really function, and people can't easily collaborate within an organization or across organizations. But trust can also be burned up.

After some business experiences, I was left wondering whether I was too trusting. My closest mentor and partner has told me the default position in business has to be to trust. To start a business requires incredible amounts of trust — trust for your investors, your partners, and your team. You can't put everything in a contract. And even if you could, it would undermine motivation. Ideally, your trust is repaid in kind.

Of course, trust can be lost, but that doesn't mean you should raise the drawbridge and man the barricades. A branch of social science called game theory says that the best strategy is "tit-for-tat." Basically, you start out trusting. If the other side reciprocates, you keep trusting. If the other side breaks faith, you stop trusting. But that is cold, hard logic. How do you make this work while maintaining your emotional balance and your sense of integrity?

Trust starts with trusting yourself. You need to see your success as stemming from your unique constellation of talents. Even if someone betrays your trust, that should not shake your faith in yourself. Once you solidify that self-trust, you need to develop a strategy and a feel for when to place your trust in others. Here are a few practical lessons I've learned:

a) Trust your own intuition. Pay heed to the red flags you see or the warning bells you hear in your interactions with others.

b) Ask questions. If something does bother you, don't be afraid to ask questions. They don't have to be accusatory, but as per the old Cold War saying, "Trust but verify."

c) Demonstrate your self-trust. Don't undercut yourself in dealings with others with what you think are harmless little self-deprecating comments. Appear confident if not cocky. Get comfortable with this even if society tells you confidence is not sexy when girls have it or that it's threatening when minorities have it.

d) Get back in the saddle. You'll make mistakes. You'll place your trust in people who don't deserve it. That's their problem. You might mistrust people who are trustworthy. Apologize from the heart and look for implicit biases. But don't lose your trust in yourself.

Demonstrate and celebrate. Honor those who have earned your trust with celebrations big and small. There is so much mistrust in our world today that it's important to recognize the people who make our businesses and our communities work.

CHAPTER 4

FLOR MELARA

My Story begins in Oakland California. I was born on July 26th, 1990, in San Francisco, California. Three months after I was born, we moved to Oakland, California, where I've spent the rest of my life living, working, and pretty much just being a Bay Area girl.

I love my city. However, I've seen it drastically change in the last ten years, in many ways for the better, but it is also sad to watch a lot of the Oakland natives from my area moving away due to gentrification, the new high cost of living here in the Bay Area, as well as other situations.

I come from a Salvadorian family, so at home I would speak Spanish, and at school I learned to speak English. I remember really liking school, and I have enjoyed it ever since. I can recall, even when I was very young, learning so much from my teachers and being very engaged in all of my classes. I always liked going to school, so it became a big part of my life. I attended only public schools in Oakland. In high school I transferred to a charter school, which was very small, and that's where I received my high school diploma.

The day after I graduated, I knew I wanted to start in community college for two years then transfer to a four-year university. So I followed my plan and did all the general education classes at a community college. I began to realize noticed that I was very much into math, so I decided I would follow a career in math—architecture. Architecture seemed like something interesting, and it combined the best of two things I enjoy doing, art and math.

After my two years in community college I transferred to the Academy of Art University in San Francisco, where I started in the fall of 2010. I did not know anyone or anything, being the first one in my family to go to college. Though I didn't have help from anyone, and I just knew I had to do it myself, nothing was going to stop me because I wanted to graduate from college.

After my first semester I realized architecture was not the career choice I wanted. Although I didn't know what to do next, I didn't want to drop out of the Academy of Art University because I had already been admitted. I decided to study communications instead. As I started taking editing and photography classes, I became really passionate about the work I was doing. Even though I wasn't very good at it, I enjoyed it. I added camera classes as well. Because the communications department was new, a lot of our classes had teachers who were "testing" the classes on us—so while that was good in a way, I felt the classes could have been a lot more than what they were. However, through my classes, I discovered how to tell a story—either through print, digital media, television, radio, or just in person—using the communication tools I had learned.

The skills I developed also helped me to get a six-month internship in the fall of 2014 at a company called Joyous, which is where I really started to get into production and communications. I was an audio-recording assistant and did set design for an e-commerce company that was selling beauty products and fashion clothing. I learned so much from that internship. Even though I worked forty hours a week, I didn't get paid for it, but I got great experience and met wonderful videographers, producers, and other professionals.

After graduating with my bachelor's degree from the Academy of Art University, I began looking for jobs in the Bay Area, in everything from production houses to broadcast television. I applied for whatever I could find but didn't get my first job until nine months after I graduated. I kept knocking on doors, visiting companies, and just going personally to speak to human resource departments and hiring managers to see if they had looked at my resume. My efforts helped me a lot and made me very aware that I had to look for opportunities, find them, and persist until I actually found something I really liked.

In December of 2015, I still hadn't found a job, but I had my student loans to pay, so I decided to start driving Uber. The very first day I did that, I got a call from the executive producer at Univision, which is Spanish media, and she asked about the positions I had applied for. I was so excited! A week later I had an interview at Univision, and I decided to go for a production position, which was a full-time creative services producer.

I accepted the position, and from the first day I started, it was an extremely hard job. I only got one day of training, and then I just had to do the best I could with the resources I had and with little other information. But little by little I started learning the process — even though I felt at first I never would learn it!

At the same time I started working at Univision in February of 2016, I had already enrolled in a master's program from Syracuse University. This was a Master of Science and Communications with a focus on advertising. I started two months after I was hired at Univision, learning not only my work responsibilities but also my schooling. It was very hard because I worked from three in the morning until noon, and then I would attend classes from two in the afternoon until six in the evening. It was definitely a tough year.

I worked hard, and the following year I finally received my master's degree. At Univision, the executive producer position became vacant in July of 2017, and I was chosen as a good candidate for the position.. A few months before, I decided to stay with the company, on the condition that I be on camera for the show I was producing. That day I got the opportunity to do so, and I've been on-camera talent as well as an executive producer of the company ever since.

I am the leader of a team of four people, all who are much older than me. Leadership has taught me much and has made me realize you can get to where you want to go as long as you have the mindset for it and prepare yourself for what's coming. Failure is going to happen, but you have to be ready for it. If you get back up and keep going, nothing can stop you.

As an executive producer, I am currently in charge of a morning show. It includes sports, technology, entertainment, health, and wellness and fitness. I am in charge of putting together the entire show, working very closely with the sales department to create sellable content that clients can take advantage of to address our audience in the Bay Area about the products or the services they offer.

It's been a very rewarding job because I've been able to work with different departments, learning the different protocols involved with each of them. I've also found out what it means to be hands-on and on your feet at all times, ready for whatever can go wrong and available to fix a situation as necessary. Often, many fires are happening at the same time, and you have to know which fire you're going to put out first.

We went from having a team of nine people to only four, and now we've been able to do way more with just those four than when we had nine! This really speaks to the work we've been able to accomplish as well as the strategies and mindset I've established with the team. I think it's important that a person be able to do more than just one thing. A person today in my company can wear many hats: producer, on-camera talent, editor, videographer, and storyteller. We shouldn't rely on somebody else to do something when we live in the age of "do it yourself." We can also learn something we want to do, practice it, and put it into action without complaining. Don't expect someone else to do your job because times have been hard in many industries, such as television, that have been affected by social media and the digital age.

However, because so much of the population is focused on social media, I've made it a priority to keep my focus on social media, on what's changing, and how I am going to change with the times. It's about adapting and evolving to this new age so I can stay current in a digital age and create content attractive to a younger generation, with similar interests. I would say find your community and passionately work to inform, engage, and communicate with that tribe.

Principles and Strategies for Leadership:

The first leadership principle I want to share is to lead by example. I think we hear this more than we actually understand it. It's a phrase that's been tossed around quite a bit. In the Bible, it says you shall know them by their fruit, and this is speaking about the fruit of the Spirit. If you haven't read the Bible, then you may not understand what I'm talking about, but people will reveal themselves based not their words but their actions. So if somebody says, "I'm hard-working," but their actions don't demonstrate that, then they're not really hard-working. That's how you get to know people.

Another familiar phrase is regarding people who "talk the talk but don't walk the walk." To be respected, be someone who is true to what you say. In other words, show who you are by your actions and not so much by your words. The verse I mentioned says you shall know them by their fruit— and it's true you may say you are one thing, but what you actually show yourself to be is completely different. It even defines who you are. That's one of the biggest things that as a leader you need to do: be who you say you are. You might say you're a great hard-working leader who leads by example, but do you really do that? Remember that you have people you're influencing, who are watching the way you behave. I say this because I've struggled with it myself, and I believe it's always best to be honest with yourself and fix the things you do not like. I want to you to understand that many of the principles I'm sharing are examples of mistakes I've made and that I continue to work on day to day. If you're not willing to look at yourself in the mirror and accept your errors and failures, it will be very hard to grow, personally and professionally. Don't just say things to make yourself appear better than you are.

As a leader you want to be the first one who takes ownership of not just your words but also the work you're doing, making sure that if you're in the forefront of a team, you are the first one taking action, you're the first one doing what you said everyone else should do. That would be my first leadership principle.

My second leadership principle is to value your time and the time of those around you. It might sound like something that's very easy, but it's actually one of the hardest things to do when you're a leader. You are a very busy person, but that doesn't mean you spend every second of your day doing actual "work." You also must read books, make plans, devise schedules, and meet with people. What that means is that you know how you've assigned your day or your week or your month, and you need to value that. And not just value your own time, but also value the time of those around you, whether it's a coworker, a business partner, somebody you are learning from, or somebody who is learning from you, which means you're not just in the spur-of-the-moment. You have to plan ahead.

We sometimes say, "I don't have the time. I need to manage my time better." Our day just goes by so fast, and before we know it, the day is gone. One thing we must understand is that life is not just about time, it's about what you do with your time and whether what you're doing is valuable to you. Many times, we make plans and accept invitations to do things that are not valuable to us. And when something is not valuable to you, sometimes you're going to be upset because you decided to do something else simply because somebody invited you to do it, maybe even forced you to do it, but you really didn't want to. So in order to value your time you need to value other people's time, and one of the best ways to do this is by saying no. Saying no is probably one of the hardest things to do because we're very used to saying yes, agreeing to things even before they happen. This is a bad thing to do because you just become an emotional person, and in the spur of the moment, in the emotion or joy of the moment, you decide to say yes without actually knowing what you're saying yes to. If it is hard for you right now to say no, then just say, "I don't know." *I don't know* is a great second option that can get you out of a lot of situations and help you value your time and the time of those around you.

My third principle is to be heard as a leader. It's important that you're being heard, not just by the team but also by your other coworkers, your managers, and your company. What this means is that you are voicing your opinions and you're not just watching others get to where they want to be but you're also saying, "How am I going to get where I want to be? What will I have to do or say?" This is huge, because it's not always easy to voice your opinion, especially when you're new or young or seeking a position that ten other applicants want too.

It's tough to voice your opinion and needs because you fear you might get fired for it, but I think it's very important. If we're not heard, we're just going to watch other people voice their needs and get what they want; we'll stay in the same place and end up very frustrated. For example, when I was seeking to be on camera, I told my company I would only stay as a producer if I got to be on camera. Although I was afraid to say it, and it certainly wasn't pleasant to say, I knew I had to risk it because if I didn't voice my opinion and say what I wanted, I was going to stay in a position I wouldn't enjoy.

So it's always important as a leader to make sure you're heard by upper management, by your team, and by your coworkers, even in other departments. If not, you're going to regret it, and it's better to risk it to get what you want than to not be heard and stay in the same place.

My fourth principle is to question workplace ideas, regulations, protocols, and guidelines or rules. What do I mean by this? I mean that when people establish a certain set of guidelines, we tend to think of those guidelines or rules as the way things have to be. But the way people work today is changing, and so we must question different rules and regulations. We must ask why we do certain things in certain ways. You're not always going to get a very pleasant answer, and most times people won't even know the answer. They'll just say, "Because so and so did it this way," or "Because it's always been done this way," or "That's just the way it is." But it's always important to question people. If somebody tells you can't do it that way, ask them, "Why can't I do that?" Ask where this rule is written down—"Is it a company policy? If it is, can you tell me why?" It's always great to question the way things are done and also understand why they're done that way, this will help you to not only keep your eyes open for things that might not go with your values and whatever you consider valuable in your life, but also to question just different ideas and things you're not in agreement with.

My next principle is an important one because it's about how you treat other people. The way we treat other people will always have an impact, whether it be negative or positive. It's important that we treat people with respect but also that we understand that the way we treat others speaks a lot about who we are. Maybe you think you're treating someone with respect, but if you are looking down on somebody because you are a manager or a leader, and you're treating them like they're below you because they are just workers, just employees, well, at the end of the day, the way you treat others is really going to speak about you and not so much about them. So I think this is very important because whether you are an executive producer or in an upper management position, the way you treat others will always speak about you. It can either be good or it can be bad, but it will never be neutral, so we must make sure that we treat others the way we want to be treated.

My next principle is to reevaluate your "why." This is very important because sometimes you don't even know why you're doing things, and you don't know what your goals are. I think it's important to reevaluate your why every six months. I would say that knowing your why—why you're in that position, why you're in that job, why are you forcing yourself to do something—is very important. Some people's whys may be because they want more money, because they want to get a better position, because they want to start their own business. Whatever your why is, always make sure that you know what it is and that it's getting you closer to your goal because sometimes you get lost in the motions and the daily routines and you forget your goal: Why are you there?

Maybe you're not at the job you want to be, but that's okay because you're there for a reason. If nothing else, it is to get you to the next step. No one can jump from step 1 to step 20. You have to go from step 1 to 2 to 3 to 4. Maybe you can skip a step here and there, but you're not going to get from 1 to 10 or 1 to 20 in one step. You have to take small turns, you have to take small steps, and one of the ways in which you're going to do it successfully is by evaluating your why. You need to understand why you're doing what you're doing to hit your goal of being where you want to be.

My next point is attitude. A great quote I heard once said, "The attitude you bring to the day will be what the day will bring to you." A great attitude will bring a great day. It's very true that when you have a positive attitude, when you have an contagious attitude, then you start spreading your positive attitude towards somebody else. This is important because the attitude we take towards the things that happen to us in our everyday life is what's going to determine what we'll receive from that day. So when it comes to attitude, we have to have not only a positive attitude but also an achieving attitude, an attitude that wants more, an attitude that wants to receive something great, something big, and based off of that, you're going to bring that to the day.

My next point is leadership. A lot of people are entering the leadership world, but what makes them leaders and what is going to keep them being leaders is a willingness to fail. I think one of the greatest quotes I've heard is that a leader will fail and will mess up, but he will still keep leading. That's true! Just because you're a leader doesn't mean you're perfect and you won't make mistakes. What it means to be a leader is that you're going to learn from your mistakes, get back up, and continue leading and giving orders (or delegating), if that's what you were called to do. You will continue creating strategies, building businesses, teaching people, creating other leaders, teaching new strategies, and creating better businesses.

But being a leader doesn't mean you're the only one in control and that you've never failed. It means that because you're in control, you're going to fail, but you're going to keep yourself in control, and you're going to keep yourself telling people and guiding those who are with you to be better leaders themselves. I think one of the best ways to become a leader is to lead by example, which I said before, but also to understand that leadership is not about being perfect, and it's not about not making mistakes. It's about making mistakes and learning from them and continuing to be a leader. It doesn't matter if you mess up, it doesn't matter if your plan did not go as you thought it would. You risked it, and you didn't care, and you continued to lead.

My next point is passion. If you don't know what you're passionate about, don't be afraid to find out. There is no passion without love, so whatever you're passionate about, you have to love it, and if you don't know what you love, then don't worry too much. You can find out by understanding what it is that you do day by day. What is it that you like to look at? What is it that you would like to understand more about? What is it that you like to work on?

These things are going to show you who you are and what you like. They will show you your passion.

Once you find that, understand that whatever it is, it's not necessarily going to be easy to make a good living from that passion, but it's a good place to start, just by learning what it is you love. When you do something you love, you're not doing it because other people are doing it. You're not doing it because it's a trend or because it's popular at the moment. You're doing it because it's what you love and what you are passionate about. That is a huge advantage over somebody who's doing something just because they see other people doing it or just because they are focusing on making money. Making money is not the same as passion. You can be very passionate about making money, but you can't make money by just pretending to be passionate about something. You have to truly love what you're doing in order to be passionate.

And my final leadership advice is to risk it. Don't be afraid to risk it! It's always a good thing to risk it, whether you risk losing your job or risk getting a new job or even risk starting a new business. Just go for it! It's not always going to be the best, you might lose a lot of money, or you might make a ton—but at the end of the day, if you don't risk it, you're never going to know. This is probably one of the biggest things that leaders are doing — taking the risk.

By taking the risk, I don't mean to impulsively make decisions out of nowhere. I mean that if it's what you want to do, if it's what's tugging at your heart, and what you've already researched (in its entirety), then do it. Otherwise, you will never know what could have been. Risk going for that job. Risk taking that role and just going for it because that's what matters, and that's what you need to do. Go for what you want. Risk it, and know that even if it doesn't turn out the way you wanted it to turn out, you did it anyway. That will give you the wings of freedom and a sense of risk that is incomparable, and this will inspire you to do more.

Have you ever done something you were very much afraid to do? How did you feel afterward? It's sort of like a scary roller coaster that you're too afraid to get on. Once you do get on it, you realize it wasn't so bad after all, and you're even willing to give it another go.

CHAPTER 5

MARILU GONZALEZ

I was born in La Piedad, Michoacán, Mexico, on a Friday night, and my parents named me Maria Luisa Gonzalez. Little did they know that they would travel to Harvey, Illinois, and there I would be renamed as Coach Marilu. I have a phenomenal family. I have four brothers and two sisters, and we know hardship very well. My mother raised us alone in poverty after the death of my father. My father was stricken with cancer. He fought as hard as he could, and he even lived longer than everyone thought he would; the doctors told him he had three months, and he fought for three years.

My father's death was devastating, yet his legacy of a champion mindset has been the inheritance we have passed on to our own children. My mother was a self-proclaimed community activist and a church leader. It was not abnormal for me to be volunteering at a church or at a pantry in middle school. It was the norm in my family, regardless if there was abundance or not.

My grandmother was the jewel of the family and my greatest cheerleader. It was my grandmother's love and validation that motivated me to go to college, and soon I became a first-generation college grad. She gave me the nerve to be fearless, to be curious, and to explore the realm of education. The motto for our family has always been that education is the key. My seven brothers and sisters are all professionals. Cumulatively, we've accomplished five bachelor's and six master's degrees in math, Spanish, English, early childhood education, physical education, EL, behavior specialists, and educational leadership. My siblings' work ethic shows that their accomplishments are phenomenal.

My brother Jose, or Coach Tony, has been inducted into the NJCAA hall of fame, and my brother David is now the head coach for both the girls' and the boys' high school teams. My brother Jesse is a high school soccer coach as well. My sister Gini works at an elementary school within our community. I have spent eleven years of my career as a teacher and a coach, building a competitive women's soccer program and teaching swimming at Thornton High School. I have been part of the soccer community since 1994, and I was the head coach for both the high school district and South Suburban College, which both my brothers took over after my promotion as an administrator.

When I was a teenager, you could find me playing at the local park with my family or traveling every Sunday to watch soccer games. At a young age I found comfort in the sense of belonging that a team could provide and in the opportunity to practice leadership skills. Soccer became my passion. Teaching is my love, coaching is my life, and leadership is my calling. I graduated from Chicago State University and Concordia University-Chicago and earned a bachelor's in science and physical education and a master's in arts and educational leadership, respectively.

My education career started at Northern Illinois University, where I received a scholarship, and I was able to start my career with pre-med, which then evolved to athletic training, then to teaching. I had phenomenal professors. I had opportunities. I fell in love with education. I fell in love with knowledge. I fell in love with the way that people were so passionate about their craft, how they got so detailed about their content. So as I committed to my district,

I was simultaneously the head coach for the girls' soccer team for ten years and head coach for South Suburban College for eight years. I would coach both in the fall and in the spring.

And in the winter, you could find me in a soccer dome, training smaller children. My first group of five-year-olds are now young men. That experience was an experience of a lifetime, both for me and for those boys. We were able to accomplish so much in such little time. But the most important part of all was the fact I was enjoying every single minute of practice, of games, of interactions with the parents, of competition at all levels. We were able to go so many places, competing at the highest levels.

My recipe was easy. I stuck to the fundamentals. I used the theory and the knowledge I accumulated in my degree. I broke it down into pieces, then I translated it to developmentally appropriate language for my boys. It worked. I used behavior management skills, and I used teaching practices. My boys were able to win national tournament championships, and most of them are in college.

You can describe my philosophy as learning skills through education and athletic experience. I believe the athletic arena is the opportunity to practice life skills. In the trajectory of my career, you can see the transformation from teaching to coaching to leadership. My career has evolved. I became the first Latino administrator in the history of my current district. I am more than a first; I am a generational change-maker for all students and teachers.

I have stated that it is not a matter of ambition for me but a strong sense of duty I feel I owe my community. We have an urgency for decision-making individuals who understand Latino students, parents, community members, and businesses at any table within all educational levels in this dynamic community. Not because it is failing, but because it is richly striving. I was elected by the teacher's spotlight as an up-and-coming leader in March 2016 by a newsletter that is published by IALAS, the Illinois chapter of the Association of Latino Administrators and Superintendents.

Here is where I made that commitment and promise to be a leader, and to make decisions that would help my community. In 2017 I was hired as an additional layer of administration, as a division leader for physical education, health, driver's education, and family and consumer science (FACS). There my mission has been to propel the district's vision and create an environment where students can erase the classroom walls and connect what they are learning to the real world. I've thus far hired four new teachers, three of which have thousands of hours in industry experience. They bring into our high school the entrepreneur mindset.

I'm currently helping them marry best-teaching practices with their business sense. My experience with AVID strategies, IB principles, quantum learning, TR Silver tools, and the Danielson rubric has enabled me to become an influence for teachers, which then transpires to students. I believe innovative ideas promoted by my state board of education have been the cornerstones for my teaching and coaching methods for years. I've always incorporated socio-emotional learning skills, social justice, and cultural relevancy to my lessons as well as my signature "chalk talks."

It is the attention to that marriage between professional development and personal development that guides my work. My ambitious attitude has taken me to impressive heights in both coaching and teaching careers. I'm expected to reach those heights using the same recipe and make it a reality in my new career as an administrator. Much of my work has been centered around getting all students and parents abreast of the great opportunities in higher education. In my coaching career, I've granted thousands of athletic scholarship dollars to many students from my community.

In my internship in district 205, I was able to be part of the Illinois State Board of Education audit and draft strategic plans for groundbreaking after-school programs. My community work never stops. You can find me marching against violence or researching DACA scholarships for my present students. My work as an advocate starts with building relational capacity with my teachers and attracting resources for my students. I'm relentless in my community, and I promote diversity and cultural education in my building.

As a high school student in the same district where I have grown professionally, advocating for innovation has driven my agendas. High expectations for students and a nurturing culture are two of my priorities. Currently I am a board member for the Communications and Arts Department at Governor State University in University Park. In this role, I'm able to explore the possibilities of building ties with higher education in high school curriculum. It is here where I can have conversations with professors, which spark ideas to offer more for my students.

It is my spirit of light that I strongly believe is apparent in all my work as well as my willingness to step out of my comfort zone that has yielded great gains for my students and my community. In my first year as an administrator, I was able to see a reduction in the failure rate by 20 percent. Into the second year, believe it or not, I reduced that number by 50 percent. You will hear me humbly saying this is just the beginning and that the best is yet to come. It is my intention to generate that spark in other teachers, which to me is lighting ideas in young people. Those ideas generate a fire that will then create a culture shift where everything that is taught in physical education, health, driver's education, and FACS has validation and credibility and connects students directly to career pathways or to experiences they can then use to become better people in their homes and communities.

Education is the key. Education is found everywhere. We must advocate for it, we must fight for it, we must teach it, we must model it. Being a lifelong learner has been the biggest gift I could ever have received—the gift I got from my parents, from my grandparents, from my community. I have made a commitment to ensure sustainable systems are in place that can create opportunities for all generations to come. It is time that education is married to business and to real life.

Everything you do in school is something useful for you, and you can apply it to your life either at home, at work, in your personal life, and for growth within yourself, your family, and the community. My children have been the greatest inspiration for me. They're the ones who keep me humble and keep my feet flat on the ground. They expect so much from me, and I am willing not only to share and give all that I have and all that I've learned to them but also to everyone around me.

My children have high expectations for themselves. They also have high expectations for us as a family, and the future is brighter than ever. That's how all families should be. That's how all children should walk, with confidence, with light, with a bright future, with hope for the best, with innovation, with creativity. My life experiences have proven it to be correct. You can overcome adversity. You can overcome challenges. You can create your own life. You can be the master of your own story, and the story never ends because there's so much to learn, there's so much to do, and there's so much to create. Education is the key.

Leadership Principles

It has been my experience that leadership is not easy, so in building principles within your career and the trajectory of your passion, you need to make sure that, with all else, you identify yourself. Your identity must be solid, have meaning, and be easily definable, and you should be able to go back to that foundation every step of the way.

Leadership principles are built on the experience you have. You can apply many, many principles to yourself, but not all of them are going to be relevant to what you're doing at every moment. You have to be able to integrate these principles into your character, into your everyday work, into the interactions between you and other people. It's important that you don't rely just on the principles to justify the direction in which you take your projects, the way you spend your budget, or how you prioritize your daily tasks. Make them practical.

Some of the principles that have helped me have been very simple. Even though we can get as complicated as we want when we work, when we're dealing with challenges or when we're problem-solving, creating initiatives, or creating projects, we can get very complicated. But to me, the leadership principles that have helped me have been the simplest ones.

1. Put love first.

Everything you do, you must love. Everything you complete, you must love. That's just the bottom line.

Don't do anything you don't love. Don't do anything you're not going to have passion for. Don't do anything you're not going to be willing to refine the details, that you're not going to be willing to spend time on — maybe even more time than you originally thought. It may take some research. It may take rewriting action plans. It may take advocating for resources. Or it may take talking to people — people who are more successful than you, people in the community, or business owners. You must love what you're doing to be able to sacrifice all that time, thought, and energy to it.

2. Don't compromise your dignity.

I don't do anything if I have to compromise my dignity, if it's something I'm not going to be proud of or if it's something I am not going to want to share with everybody. It doesn't matter who it is for — if it's my son, my brother, my sister, or a friend — I don't do anything that compromises my dignity, and I practice that.

That's a leadership principle I believe people sometimes feel that they can manipulate or put on pause or put in their back pocket. They think it's okay for them not to feel proud of what they're doing or to feel that compromised is normal. I don't believe in that at all. Being uncomfortable and being compromised are two totally different things. I believe that, no matter what, you must keep your dignity in the forefront, and you have to wear it every day. In other words, you have to go back to it at every moment, in every conversation, in every debate. You have to be able to repeat what you're doing over and over again to everyone, confident in knowing you are creating things that are transparent, honest, and have substance.

3. You must be able to drive through adversity.

One of the principles of leadership is the ability to take on extremely difficult challenges, even those challenges other people shy away from. You must be willing to do the extra work other people don't want to do, having that extra conversation no one wants to have. The courageous conversations I've had have taken sometimes up to six months to resolve, constantly going back to the problem, strategizing through it, being consistent, and staying the course. It has been extremely important for me to be able to do that.

4. You must commit.

The principle of overcoming adversity has its own cliché. Many times, people shy away or give up those hardships and problems to other people, or they assume it's not their responsibility. As a leader, you must understand that the principle of commitment should be worn every day. When you wake up in the morning, and you're getting ready to go to work, you need to remember that you don't have a right to give up on your commitment because you took responsibility for that leadership role. You've made that decision to be committed, and that's not something you can give up every day. It's not something you can say to yourself, "Well, today I don't feel like being committed. Today I don't feel like being in love. Today I'm not going to have dignity. And today I don't want to overcome adversity."

All these principles are a commitment. It's a commitment to the people whom you're serving. It's a commitment to the business where you're working. It's a commitment to bring the best of yourself into the spaces that are being allowed to you and for the people whom you're working for. These leadership principles are extremely important to model for the people who are following your lead.

To me, these are simple principles to follow. I've always reiterated how important it is to have personal development. I think after being a leader now for a couple of years, I've realized that my personal development has helped me so much more in this new career path I've taken than any professional development I've had. My personal development has brought me to where I am and has taken me to successful routes, not only for myself and my family but also for the community I'm working for. I've built a way of thinking. It's a paradigm shift, a change in culture, a change in environment. Your influence, which you bring into that environment, has made an impact, and that impact you've made has come to light because of the leadership principles you've committed to. Love, dignity, and overcoming adversity are principles that may seem simple, but they've done so much for me.

5. Giving back.

The last principle I believe in is giving back—being able to teach other people to make that commitment, to love what they do, to find their passion, to have dignity. When you give back to others, you have those conversations where you can explore those ideas and share examples of things you've done that describe having dignity and overcoming adversity.

Sharing and giving back is extremely important. If you don't take the time to give back to people, you may find that you don't feel complete in the work you do. You can love what you do, you can have dignity, you can overcome adversity, and be committed, but if you don't give back, it seems like the circle is always going to be open, and something's going to be incomplete.

A leader works all the time. A leader is on the job seven days a week, 24-7, to have closure and to complete thoughts and projects. And as a leader you need to share and teach. You must continue to coach and pass along those opportunities, even creating new ones for others, opening doors or building new paths. That's giving back.

Giving back is also being grateful by going back to the people who have opened doors for you and thanking them for the opportunities.

Giving back is not only giving to younger people. I've learned that as a leader there really isn't any age or any particular group of people I can't influence. The doors have swung wide open, and opportunities have arisen for me to work with people from different age levels, backgrounds, education levels, and even career levels.

All the ideas I have make an impact on others, and I have to be willing to share what I'm doing and how I'm thinking with other people, creating opportunities for them too. You must be ready to give others time, energy, and resources, even helping to make connections for them and sustaining those over time. You can't lose your track or get stuck in your office for hours and days and not make and give back those connections.

The leadership principles that have worked for me have been the simplest ones. I believe it has taken a lot of experience, a lot of life lessons, and a lot of learning to understand it's the free and simple things that have enriched me and helped me to influence others. They have propelled me into circles I've never been in, led me to conversations I wouldn't have had otherwise, and motivated me to make connections with various groups of people.

At the end of the day, the leadership principles that will work for you are the ones that you are willing to commit to, to work on, to read about, and to implement, such as learning new coping skills or implementing some type of repertoire of behaviors that you can then repeat over and over again.

Finally, this is not a leadership principle but is something that has been a path for me: spirituality. Building my faith has been extremely important for me, and it has been the golden seal of my leadership experience. Without building my faith, without carrying the chains of doubt, without exploring that of myself, I believe I would not have become a leader in the first place. The challenge of being able to step into the dark, create a spark, make a light, and then have that light grow stronger and bigger and be passed on to other people has been something I know I've only been able to do because of my faith.

CHAPTER 6

MIROSLABA "LILI" VELO

Before you are a leader, success is all about growing yourself.
When you become a leader, success is all about giving others.

—Jack Welch

Who we are is how we lead.

—Brene Brown

When we think of the word *leader*, we probably think of politicians, CEOs, or people who have traditionally held positions of power. However, as I reach my forties, I have come to a deep understanding that being a leader has nothing to do with power — that is, external power.

As I was invited to write a chapter in this book on the topic of leadership, I found myself thinking about what to write. Ovidilio Vasquez, the founder of Top Leadership Experts, was once a student in my class, and now I felt like his mentee! I had been a teacher for more than ten years before I transitioned into my current position of assistant principal of an urban high school in one of the most diverse cities in the country. I thought, *Well, perhaps that is what makes me a leader.* But that was too easy of an answer — roles don't necessarily make a person a leader. I continued to reflect on the concept of leadership. I thought about my life, the challenges that have enabled me to grow, the reading I had recently immersed myself in, and the podcasts I had been listening to. And I came to the following conclusion about leadership: a leader is one who is always unfolding and honoring their purpose in life. In doing so, a leader inspires others and takes great responsibility in the self-development of others.

My story begins in the city of Arvin, California, a small rural city in the outskirts of Bakersfield, California, where the main street is about two miles long with three stoplights. It is a migrant community, mostly farm workers from Mexico and the children of Okies and Arkies, as they were historically called. I was the firstborn of four children. My parents did not speak English. My father migrated to this country in his early thirties without a formal education from Mexico. He was a farm worker, while my mother stayed home. Although I did not know it at the time, we grew up in abject poverty, living in Section-8 housing subsidized for agricultural workers. I remember looking at my father's paycheck when I was in high school to learn that he made $4.25 an hour—what amounted to be about $450 every two weeks. The financial insecurity my parents faced caused stress and tension in their relationship, and they did not have the skills necessary to navigate the conflict that arose. Instead of looking forward to going home when school was out, I became involved in leadership and sports to avoid being home. School became my outlet; it was a way for me to escape the problems from home, find approval from my teachers, and find a sense of purpose.

I did well in school—well enough to be one of the few to leave my hometown and attend the University of California Berkeley in the summer of 2000. During high school, however, my biology teacher, Mr. Moore, informed me of a summer program called the NASA Sharp Plus Program in which high school students from all over the country were sent to different universities to conduct research for about six weeks. I was selected and found myself traveling outside of California, for the first time, to the University of Wisconsin, Madison. I would be working with a researcher at the university's hospital to try to find a cure for organ transplant patients whose body was rejecting the new organ. I still vividly remember one defining moment while I was there: the opening of my first email account. What stood out was the fact that while I sat there staring at the directions on the computer screen, typing one letter at a time with my two index fingers, my peers were typing at what seemed to me the speed of light, using all their fingers.

I was dumbfounded. I felt inadequate. I started to notice how my life was different in comparison to my peers. While I was at the top of my class at my high school (I graduated salutatorian), I soon realized that my peers were exposed to so much more—private tennis lessons, chess, reading for pleasure, alternative rock music (I listened to Banda el Recodo and Boyz II Men), and running to stay healthy. Who knew?! I remember agreeing to a run by the lake with my roommate, not knowing that it would turn out to be a five-mile run! Running a mile while conditioning for volleyball season back at home was an accomplishment for me.

The following year I applied again at the prompting of Mr. Moore and was sent to Hampton University in Virginia—this time as the student leader of the cohort. Hampton was so different from Madison; within the first few hours of arriving I started to question the program's decision to send me there and wanted to return home. This was different, and I felt uncomfortable. I finished the program nonetheless, and the next summer I found myself heading to the University of California at Berkeley, this time as a real college student.

Cal is where it all began for me. It was the beginning of my awakening process. It is where I began to understand my world and my lived experiences. I took classes on race, education, environmental politics, history, public policy, yoga, and even meditation. I traveled. I did an internship at the capital. I was *deep* in the learning of myself. I loved it so much I decided to stay a fifth year! But there were moments of doubt, especially at the beginning.

I now understand that if it had not been for my participation in the NASA Sharp Plus Program, my transition to Cal would have been a lot more difficult, not only for me but for my family as well.

Working at a bridal shop during the last few weekends before I made my journey to Cal, I managed to save $400. It was that $400, a one-way ticket on the Amtrak from Bakersfield to Berkeley, and spending the night with a Cal student who had graduated from my high school two years before I did that allowed me to check in the next day to Cal's summer transition program, Summer Bridge. This program prepared me for the academic rigor of Cal. It focused on preparing students who were the first in their family to attend college or receive Pell Grants — in other words, students from low-income, under-resourced, and marginalized communities.

The thought of watching TV never crossed my mind. The world, for all I know, came to a standstill, except for what happened between the dormitory I stayed in, the classrooms where I had my classes, the tutoring center at the Chavez Center, and Telegraph Avenue, where once in a while I could indulge in a slice of pizza from The Slice. My first semester at Cal I enrolled in three major courses: calculus; education, taught by Jeff Andrade-Duncan (now the founder of Roses in Concrete Charter School in Oakland); and chemistry. I barely managed to pass my chem class with a C minus, but my discussion leader sent me an email when the semester ended asking me out on a date! (I always wondered if that is why I barely passed that class!) Yet, I had survived, even with doubts of belonging at such a prestigious university.

My defining moment as a student at Cal, however, was when I was asked to give the keynote speech to the 2005 Summer Bridge graduates at their end-of-program celebration. That summer I had become a discussion leader for one of the ethnic studies classes, and since they knew I was a graduate of the program, I was approached to speak. In retrospect, it continues to affirm for me how the universe has a way of giving me what I need most when I most need it. Although I have since lost my written speech, my intention was to acknowledge what I assumed they were feeling—that is, that like me, when I was in their shoes, I too was going through moments of doubt, moments of questioning why I was accepted at Cal, but I had learned that because of my experiences, I had a unique voice. It was a voice that needed to be shared and was just as necessary as the voices of the students who would be soon joining them in the fall semester. When I finished my speech, I received a long-standing ovation. I knew I had connected with each one of the students sitting in the audience. In giving back, I had received so much more—I did not realize then that I too needed to hear my speech.

When I graduated, I went on to become a teacher, hoping I could continue to share my zeal for learning and inspire students who reflected my experiences to attend college. I loved every moment of teaching (except, perhaps, grading stacks of essays!). I plunged deep into my work, staying late nights prepping on my lesson plans. I was lucky enough to have joined the Words that Made America Program at the Alameda County Office of Education. Avi Black directed the program and provided me with the opportunity to reflect and grow as a teacher at an exponential rate.

I now realize that becoming a teacher was a way for me to continually be in a space of learning. I learned so much from my students, and I am thankful for them. Now, as a mother with two kids (a three- and a five-year-old) and being married to a Nigerian, my children and my relationship with my husband have become my new teachers, and I find myself *deep* in study again, continuing to learn, challenge, and honor myself. Whether I continue as an administrator at a school or travel all over the country sharing my experiences and inspiring others to understand that to become a leader, one must first work on themselves to truly give back, I have come to understand three key principles: Know yourself. Grow yourself. Honor yourself.

I end my story with these principles that I have birthed via my own experiences. If you apply them as I have, you will undoubtedly become a great leader but, more importantly, live a fulfilled and content life.

Know Yourself

The quality of your leadership can only be as rich as the depths in which you truly know yourself. As a leader, you know what you stand for. As a leader, you can identify your values. As a leader, you are content with who you are and fully accept yourself. As a leader, you are present in the moment but also envision the future. As a leader, you deeply understand that your power comes from within you. And as a leader, you maintain your power by both honoring your divine purpose and taking great responsibility in the self-development of others.

In knowing who you are, you stand grounded like a tree with deep roots; no storm will uproot you, no matter how strong and challenging the storm may look. You stand with full confidence of the decisions you make, not because you think they will work but because if they fail, you know that failure is part of the learning process and provides you with feedback on what your next steps are. As a leader, always seek to know yourself.

Grow Yourself

If for any reason, the storm manages to tilt you to one side, create a quiet space in the storm, thank it for uncovering parts of yourself that need healing, and begin the process of making yourself whole again. You ask empowering questions such as *What is this storm trying to teach me?* And you remain curious, detaching yourself from self-judgment and focusing on allowing the emotions that come up to be fully experienced so as to avoid blocking your source of divine power. Remember that you are always unfolding, and the pain that arises during the storms allows you to become more deeply in touch with your divine purpose.

Honor Yourself

When the tree stands firm with its roots deeply planted in Mother Earth and bearing fruit, you are in sync with your divine purpose, and you are in a position to lead. At some point in your life you have in one way or another asked yourself, *What is my purpose on earth?* When you honor what has been placed in you, you live your fullest version of yourself. You radiate joy and love because you are in sync with your divine purpose. In doing so, you become a model of living your highest life and inadvertently become a leader with those you encounter.

The question is, *How do you know you are living your highest self?* You know when what you do is not defined as work but, rather, a calling. You know when you wake up in the morning eager to get your day started and find yourself awake late at night because you have lost track of time doing what you are passionate about. You know when your mind is continually seeking to learn more about your calling, and you do it because it deeply fulfills you and brings you a sense of completeness.

To end, I want to share some resources that have been instrumental in my own development as a leader:

- *Oprah Winfrey's Super Soul Sunday Conversations* (YouTube or podcast)
- Reading—lots of reading! My favorite authors are Elena Aguilera, Michael Bernard Beckwith, Brene Brown, Daniel Pink, Tony Robbins, Don Miguel Ruiz, Eckhart Tolle, and Gary Zukav.

- Journals! Use them to write down your thoughts, document your storms, reflect on yourself, list what you are grateful for, envision your future, and so on.

CHAPTER 7

OVI VÁSQUEZ

They say that luck is when preparedness and opportunity meet. So I hope you are prepared for the opportunities that will arise during and after you read this book. This book is your key for you to connect with us.

Since people connect with other people through their story, I want to share with you a little bit of my story—how I grew up, how I made it to the United States, how I learned English in the school system, and how I was able to join some of the world's largest global tech corporations, and get accepted to Harvard Business School Online.

Then I'll impart to you three simple leadership principles I believe everybody needs to consciously put into practice daily. I'll keep them short and to the point.

I grew up in a small village in Guatemala. I like to say I am a farm boy from the sugarcane fields of Guatemala. My family is small. I have a mom, a sister, and a brother; my dad was killed when I was six months old. My sister has her daughters, my brother has his sons, and I have a baby girl named Emy, who is ten months old at the time of this writing.

I was born in a small village, and we were very poor. We were so poor that, to this day, there is no running water where I was born. And as early as I can remember, we had no electricity until about the year 2000. I was always running around shoeless. Every day I would walk forty-five minutes to school and then walk back forty-five minutes. I could never afford to buy shoes in different seasons of the year, so we only had one pair of shoes for the entire year.

My mom lived with her husband, my stepfather. His name was Juan Francisco Chinchilla, and he taught me how to work in the fields planting beans, yucca, and corn. I learned how to work hard while growing up.

My grandmother (Doña Elena Sarceño Ruiz) lived close to us. She had a lot of land, on which I would work with cows. My uncle Hector was the one who taught me how to milk cows when I was eight years old. I went to the fields with him every day at five in the morning, sometimes six, depending on how early he would wake up. I did that until I was able to milk cows on my own.

Our village was very far from the town, at least a forty-minute ride by car or motorcycle. We would get to go to town about once a month. If you can imagine an isolated village very far away from the nearest town in a third-world country, this will give you an idea of how poor I grew up.

Many people in the United States complain about their lack of resources here. But in comparison, if they were to move to where I grew up, the difference would be night and day. Even if the resources are low here in the United States, the quality of life allows for opportunities.

After I grew up in the sugarcane fields, my mom decided to travel to the United States. In 1998, when I was still seven years old, she left me with my uncle to take care of me. I didn't really like it there, so I traveled back to my grandma's home so I could be raised by her. As time went by, I moved in with different people, from my grandmother to my mom's friends to some other friends to my aunts. I moved at least seven times.

This meant I also had to move schools each time. One time I was supposed to go on to third grade, but my new school thought I was coming from a school that was not up to standard, so they put me back to first grade. There I was, feeling like the smartest kid in the class because I already knew everything of this first-grade class. They still didn't put me in third grade, even though they could see that my progress was much better than the rest of the class.

When I was fifteen, I was working in the sugarcane fields, having already quit school after sixth grade. I knew that if I could make money, I didn't need to attend school anymore, so I worked every day to do just that.

In 2006, my mom called and asked me if I wanted to come to the United States to where she was living. Like most people who live in third-world countries, we dream of one day making it to the United States of America. So I embarked on the journey, through Guatemala and then Mexico, walking in the fear of the unknown—which can lead you to the place of your dreams or to the most feared place of your life—which, for most of us, is death.

The Mexican government put me in jail because they discovered I was not Mexican, and then they sent me back to Guatemala. But like most people who are aiming for a goal and don't give up, I gave it another shot. This time, with much better luck, I made it to the border of the United States, after having struggled for almost thirty days, either riding on buses, walking, or through some other means, to be able to make it to this point.

After being in Tijuana for about three days, waiting for the right day to make it to the United States, I embarked on the next journey, which was walking through the desert. The men who were going to guide us through offered us some food and water. They said we could eat it up, since we were only going to be on the path for around six to eight hours. We trusted them because they were our guides, but twelve hours later, hungry and dehydrated, we began to complain. We wondered why we were still walking when it was promised to us it would only take eight hours to reach the United States.

Our guide couldn't find where we were supposed to get to, and he confessed to us that it was his very first time guiding other people through. But I did not lose hope! My grandma instilled in me to keep praying when you want something, so I continued to pray, promising in my prayers that if I made it to the

United States of America, I was going to be a good man.

We made it to San Diego, California, after a long journey of a day and a half, walking, resting, sleeping, then walking some more through all the mountains. I was picked up at a gas station by my mom's ex-husband, who then took me to his house in Los Angeles. My mom drove from the north Bay Area of California to LA with her then-husband to pick me up.

When she arrived, I felt a level of emotion I had never felt before. I'd made it to the promised land, and I was able to see my mother, who I had not seen for many, many years. This was a moment of hope, a moment of promise.

We traveled from Los Angeles to Hayward, California, and when I arrived, my mom took me to buy some clothes at the used clothing store. Here I was, excited that I was in the United States, and yet I was taken to a store to buy clothing that was already used by somebody else. But I didn't complain about it because I was happy I had made it. I purchased a few things with money given to me by my mom, and I felt like the luckiest man on earth because at least I was not dead — there was a very real possibility I could have died through my journey.

With a smile on my face, we paid for the clothing we purchased and then drove home. A few days later, a friend of my mom's helped me get a job offloading trailers full of boxes to be distributed to the malls throughout the Bay Area of San Francisco, where I currently live. I worked in that warehouse for five years.

After a year and a half of living in America, I realized I was sick and tired of not being able to communicate with other people; I wanted to learn English. I asked my mom if she would let me go to school to be able to learn English. She said we already had an agreement that I was going to help her build a house in Guatemala, and if I were to go to school, and they were to find out I was working in a warehouse in a night shift, she would get in trouble.

Of course, I didn't want my mom to get in trouble, but the need for me to speak English was there every day. I decided to continue to ask her until she let me go to school. I enrolled in high school in March of 2008 so I could learn to speak English.

Many people told me this high school was one of the worst schools in the area, but I never paid attention because all I wanted was to learn English. I never cared about the sports or the extracurricular activities. All I wanted was to be able to speak English with anybody at any time, any day.

About a year later, my mom went back to Guatemala to take care of my dying grandmother, who had raised me. Three months later, my grandmother passed away. My mom called during my US History class to tell me. I felt like the world fell on my shoulders.

There I was, living by myself in the United States, barely speaking any English, working at a warehouse during the night, receiving the news that the person I loved the most had just passed. I felt like quitting because I couldn't handle the pain anymore. I felt weak and hopeless, like there was nothing else to aim for.

But after having a conversation with my counselor three days later, when I attempted to tell her I was going to dropout of high school, she persuaded me to stay in school. I decided to stay and work at it more than ever.

Two years later, on June 6, 2011, I graduated. It took a total of three years for me to graduate high school. As everybody was getting called up on the stage to get their diploma, their family members were cheering for them. No one from my family was there except for my aunt. I wanted to have my mom, my grandma, and my sister or brother watch me cross the graduation stage after the long three years of hard work, dedication, and persistence.

All this time, I was what people would call undocumented, so I didn't have any opportunity to find good jobs. And I didn't have guidance or a mentor or coach to show me the way, to help me find or build an opportunity.

In 2014, I received DACA, which is a permit from the government that allows undocumented young people who have a clean background to legally work and live in the United States. I took advantage of the opportunity, and with my DACA I began to work for a third-party company that had contracts with Apple. After joining with them, I became a computer technician, learning the systems Apple has for the refurbishment department.

After two years there, I applied at Tesla for hope of better pay. Tesla hired me as a technician, where I worked on the robots building the batteries they call modules. So now I was a robot technician. I didn't have money to go to college, but I did have technical experience I gained at work. After a few months at Tesla, I decided it was time for me to leave because I wanted more for myself.

This ambition in me could not let me stay in one place. I found an opportunity to go to school in San Francisco in a year-long private technical training program. When I joined that program, I was trained on computer network systems, project coordination, IT skills, and a few other things. I decided to choose project management because it was something I felt I was strong at and I wanted to leverage my own potential.

While attending that training program, I worked different jobs—in construction, selling various products to people at gas stations, working at a pizzeria, and doing whatever I had to do to be able to pay my bills and send money to my mom monthly to Guatemala. But being the creative person I am, I also decided to give motivational speeches to students in school, students who had a similar story like mine, who were English learners, who grew up in farms, who had to move from one place to another, who may have grown up without their father, and who may have gone to school without their families being around—students that could identify with my story. A little while after I began doing this, I was being paid for the presentations I was offering to the students, and this was the start of my career as an entrepreneur.

After graduating from the one-year technical program I signed up for in San Francisco, I was able to join Uber, working on their self-driving technology. I had also just completed a six-month internship at a multi-billion-dollar corporation called Salesforce, also in San Francisco.

After a couple of months working at Uber, they stopped operations, and because I didn't want to move to a different state, I decided to quit that job and take another one with a tech start-up called Cruise Automation, where I also worked on self-driving technology.

After all this time, I continued delivering motivational talks in schools. This allowed me to see how much of an impact you can make telling your own story. I read countless testimonials from students, parents, and teachers who were in my audience and sat through my presentations.

Now I have shared with you my story of how I grew up, how I made it to the United States, how I was able to get my education, and how I was able to join these big tech companies. I built my resume working at Apple, Tesla, Salesforce, Uber, and Cruise Automation (who was then acquired by General Motors, another multi-billion-dollar corporation).

I hope this inspires you to see that no matter how poor, no matter how tough, no matter what the circumstances are, there is always a chance if you stay persistent and creative and don't let bad influences into your life.

Principles

The principles I want to share with you will help you get a better idea, a better grasp, on how you can elevate your own leadership so you can achieve your personal and professional success.

Principle 1: Be Someone with Audacity

In the United States, it seems like everybody is busy with their lives. They are so busy that they don't see outside their circle, and I often hear people use the phrase "Think outside the box." I think they say that because they see everybody going on the same path, just following other people who are going in front of them, without really looking out for ideas and new ways for making things happen. So having audacity will help you as a leader to develop new systems, to bring out new results unique to what you're doing.

This book you're reading right now is part of the audacity I have of being someone who develops courage and uses persuasion to put an idea together, to influence people of power, like the other authors who shared their stories in this book. I had the audacity to ask them to join me and make this idea a reality, to make this book a powerful tool that will influence you to elevate your own game with your own natural skills.

Audacity is what's going to help you look up when everybody is looking down at the same idea, at the same process, at the same way of doing everything they've already done for years and years. Have the audacity to swim against the current of what everyone else is doing. Have the audacity to be the first one to say what you believe deep in your heart will make a difference.

Audacity will make you stand out; people will notice you are a different kind of leader, a person who they can truly see is an outlier and not like everybody else. When you do this though, prepare to get a lot of attention. But the more attention you get, the more chances you get to influence those who give you their attention.

Principle 2: Common Sense

Develop common sense. Without it, you're going to be lost in the crowd, because many people overthink everything, and they freeze. They don't act. And then as they get older, they realize they haven't done anything.

I have observed people who have more formal education than I do who come to me for advice on how to get a job. I've thought to myself, *Why is it that they don't use their common sense to talk to more people?* If someone says no, you simply go to the next one. If they don't respond via email, you simply give them a call. If the job doesn't say how much it pays, you simply call to ask. You get the idea.

A great deal of people overthink things and begin to make assumptions. If you use common sense, which is not common practice, you will gain an advantage over everyone else who simply follows the guidelines. Having common sense is knowing that some things you don't need an explanation for — you simply do them. You are an action-taker. You do something and ask questions later. Now, of course, you must be cautious about what you're doing, but you don't have to be timid about it. So common sense means not overthinking things. This will help you stay ahead of the game.

Principle 3: Be Autodidactic

When you're a leader, not everybody is willing to train you. Some people will be jealous of your natural abilities to learn and to guide and to lead and to influence others. You must be autodidactic, which means you are a self-taught person. You still might learn a great deal from others, but learn everything you can on your own.

As they say, finding is reserved for those who seek. So seek out knowledge from books, videos, podcasts, mentors, coaches, and establishments. Be the person who they see today at one level, and three days later, they notice you have grown, that something is different about you and that you are developing yourself.

Be autodidactic because you cannot always trust someone else's ability to teach you something the right way or the most effective way to save you time or get you to a result. Being autodidactic will enable you to take initiative, make plans, implement ideas, and, therefore, drive results.

I know these three principles I've shared with you will help you elevate your leadership game. I kept it short because I know life is short—and you have to get to doing something.

THANK YOU!

We appreciate all of your feedback, and we love hearing what you have to say.

We need your input to make the next version of this book and our future books even better.

Please leave us a helpful review on Amazon letting us know what you thought of the book.

Looking forward to reading your review

Thank you so much!
Martha Hernández | Estela Lopez
| Andrea Guendelman | Flor Melara | Marilu Gonzalez
| Miroslaba Velo | Ovi Vásquez

Made in the USA
Columbia, SC
03 September 2022

66469641R00086